Me,
Mom
&
Jesus

Me, Mom & Jesus

An Unlikely Love Story of Two Broken Hearts
and One Miracle-Working God

NIKKI S. WHITE

Me, Mom, & Jesus

An Unlikely Love Story of Two Broken Hearts and One Miracle-Working God

Copyright © 2024 by Nicole White

Requests for information should be addressed to:
Nikki S. White, 5799 S. Main Street, #1721, Clarkston, Michigan 48347

The events and dialogue in this story are based on the author's memory and may differ from others' recollections. Some names and details have been changed to safeguard the privacy of the individuals.

Cover design and image: Cameron Hahn and Tikistudios
Interior design: Cameron Hahn

ISBN 979-8-218-53218-5 (softcover)
First Paperback Edition
Printed in the United States of America

Dedication

To Kati Marie, my firstborn faith-keeper
and my crown's sparkling jewel, whose first breath
fanned 1,000 generations into a wildfire.

Contents

Preface		vii
Acknowledgments		vix
Chapter 1	What You Don't Know	1
Chapter 2	Cut Off	12
Chapter 3	Heart Problems	23
Chapter 4	Full Circle	32
Chapter 5	Finding a Way	42
Chapter 6	Flesh and Blood	51
Chapter 7	A Different View	62
Chapter 8	Home for Christmas	73
Chapter 9	Needle and Thread	83
Chapter 10	Accept No Imitation	94
Chapter 11	Pass It On	105
Chapter 12	Holding Hope	115
Chapter 13	Making Room	125
Chapter 14	No Regrets	135
Chapter 15	Enjoy Your Life	145
Chapter 16	Hope of Glory	155
Chapter 17	Jesus With Skin On	164
Chapter 18	Surrender	176
Chapter 19	Coming Home	186
Chapter 20	Carry On	196
Chapter 21	Letters From Home	208
Epilogue		220
About the Author		223

Preface

Growing up in church, I always believed the lie that I didn't have a salvation story.

After all, I was practically birthed in the pews and raised by two Christian parents who loved me. So what was there to tell?

More than the devil wanted me to.

When we share the truth of who Jesus is and what He's done for us, our witness defeats the enemy. There is no story on earth that Jesus can't redeem.

The recounting of my life in *Me, Mom, & Jesus* is offered to every reader in the spirit of God's love, the peace of Christ, and the unity of His church. When I set out to tell the story, I never intended to write a love letter to the church. But as the words poured out, I heard God calling His people back to their First Love.

Have you ever asked Jesus into your heart, then questioned where He was?

Did you grow up singing "Jesus Loves Me" but wondering if it was true?

Have you thought you had to earn salvation one shiny gold star at a time?

Me, too.

But the Bible offers "good tidings of great joy"[1] for all people.

Jesus Christ is alive forevermore! His Spirit lives within you, calling you back to Him. You are His; nothing can separate you from God's love.

I declare His Word over your life.

> For I am convinced that neither death, nor life,
> neither angels nor demons, neither the present
> nor the future, nor any powers, neither height
> nor depth, nor anything else in all creation will
> be able to separate us from the love of God that
> is in Christ Jesus our Lord.[2]

Jesus loves you. This I know. Receive the grace of God.

Your sister in Christ,
Nikki S. White

---

[1] Luke 2:10 (KJV).

[2] Romans 8:38-39 (NIV).

Acknowledgments

My offering of this book is accompanied by my undying love and inexpressible gratitude to the following people:

Jesus Christ, my Savior and the Savior of the world, who rescued this prissy, self-righteous Sunday School girl and set her feet on the solid ground of His Word. I'm not worthy, but You say I'm worth it. I'm forever Yours; You're forever mine.

My tenacious mother, Lynn, who loved me more than I knew, taught me more than I realized, and showed me more faith in five days than most people demonstrate in a lifetime.

My sweet dad, Warren, whose faithfulness and unwavering devotion to God and family have proven unshakable.

My big-hearted husband Chuck, who generously loves me like Jesus does, lays down his life for our family on a daily basis, and challenges me to embrace my imperfections and the lavish grace of God. For the record, I asked *you* to marry *me* and I'm so glad I did.

My treasured children, Kati and Chapin, the best parts of me—my hope, my love, my joy, my crown. You continue to live out your lives in ways that inspire and humble me to the core. I see Jesus in you.

My precious granddaughters, Avi and Livi. May "Jesus Loves Me" ring forever true in your hearts, and may you sing His love over your children and your children's children until we all gather to sing those words again on the day of Jesus Christ, our Lord.

My faithful son-in-law Billy, who, without a doubt, is an answer to Nanny's prayers.

My extended family members who appeared in these pages—Josh, Holly, Uncle Henry, Uncle Donnie, Grandma Melody, Barb, Deb, and Aunt Sharon. Plus those who are captured here not in words but in spirit—the Bliss, Hurwitz, and Melody families. Together, you've helped me grasp how wide, long, high, and deep is the love of Christ.

My A-team cheerleaders, Angie, Cameron, Sande, and Valerie, whose love lifted me high when I was heavy.

My pastor Tom and his dear wife, Debbie, along with the late Shirli and Don Humphreys, who were quiet voices of truth and grace that spoke into my life.

My prayer warrior tribe who were always willing to drop to their knees at a moment's notice to fight on my behalf, Angie B., Karen, Laurie, Pam, Penny, Sally, Sherre, and Wilma.

My gifted friends, Cameron Hahn, Mindy Kiker, J.B. Wilson, Ginny Yttrup, and Tikistudios, who came alongside me to lend their God-given creative talents and editing expertise as I brought this message to life.

My people, Mom's people, and God's people—the Sunday School teachers, pastors, evangelists, BSF leaders, prayer partners, nursery workers, ushers, camp cooks, and janitors who surrounded me, prayed over me, loved me, cared for me, and poured God's Word into me week after week, year after year. To fully express my thanks, eternity is required.

Chapter 1

What You Don't Know

I thought I'd give anything to regain the "good daughter" title I'd lost. Never in my wildest dreams did I imagine trying to get it back would cost someone else their life.

"Hello, Nikki?" My mother's voice was softer than usual over the phone, her words slow and deliberate. This wasn't good. "Mother. . .Grandma Melody . . . She died . . . Last night."

"Oh, Mom. I'm so sorry." I emphasized my syllables to compensate for my lack of emotion. I had none. I barely knew my mother's mother, but I did know the proper etiquette. "When's the funeral? I'll book a flight today."

Chicago was only a car ride away from our tiny Michigan town, but a flight would be quicker and less painful for all parties involved. Beyond those details, Mom and I didn't have too much to say to each other.

"Oh, man," Chuck said when I told him. "I'm sorry, Nik. Do you want me to go with you?"

I shook my head at my husband. "No, that's OK. I know work's busy. I'll take the kids. You stay."

Mom and Dad had decided to join our flight, so it'd be easier

1

on me with my husband out of the equation. I envied him; he had a good excuse not to go. Unfortunately for me, the funeral of your mother's mother was one of those nonnegotiable obligations in life.

* * *

I lugged my suitcase up the steps from the tarmac, taking up the rear of my little family's caravan. Chuck usually got us on the plane, and it was a harder job than he had made it look.

I took a deep gulp of fresh July air before stepping into the narrow aisle of a too-crowded two-propeller plane. *Just breathe. Stay calm. The canned air will kick on. This will all be over soon.* My coaching didn't calm my racing heart. I felt I had to get out of there. Now. Every cell in my lungs demanded I turn, shove strangers aside, and pop my head back outside for air.

But what about my kids? My daughter was thirteen, and my son was only eight. Would they survive a plane ride without me? Would any of us survive this trip at all?

The thought triggered a memory of a call I'd taken at work years before, as if it were yesterday. "Did you hear about that plane crash at Metro? The puddle jumper? Janie was on it." Janie was a co-worker I knew only in passing, but her death launched a fear in me that I didn't think I had. People live, and then they die. How sad it is that, in the end, you barely knew them at all, as I barely knew my grandmother.

That was not going to be the case with me. I took another deep breath and closed my eyes, feeling dizzy. God willing, my kids would know their mother. I was determined they'd never be ashamed of me or wonder if I loved them. So, how would they feel if their mom started acting like a crazed lunatic clawing her way over the seats? *Just breathe. Stay calm. The air will kick on. This will all be over soon.*

My parents were seated in the row before us, buckled in and

holding hands. Mom's face lit up when she saw her grandchildren coming toward her, then fell when she saw me taking up the rear. I pretended not to notice.

"Hi, Mom, Dad. You're here early." I smiled brightly, holding my expression through the comment that inevitably came.

"And you're late," Dad said with a smile, as if he was joking. He might have cut me some slack if he knew how much I loathed twiddling my thumbs on a plane when I could be doing something productive.

"Not late enough," I said under my breath. Secretly, I'd hoped to miss the flight and call in my condolences.

The kids and I settled into seats arranged in a broken row of three, one single and two together. I smiled across the aisle at my children's wide, innocent eyes. "Are you guys okay?" I reached across the aisle and squeezed their hands. Then, feeling generous with my emotions now that I couldn't turn back and the plane could go down, I grabbed Mom's shoulder and gave it a little shake. She reached up to hold my hand, but I'd already pulled it away.

This will all be over soon.

* * *

Entering the funeral parlor, I spotted three seats in the third row from the front, positioned to the left of the casket. Having seen me walk in with the deceased's daughter, the funeral director was quick to draw near and discreetly point out my error. "The front two rows are reserved for family," he said, barely moving his lips.

You could have fooled me. Most of the people in the room looked less than vaguely familiar, though I knew Mom's two younger brothers, Uncle Henry and Uncle Donnie. My own little brother, Josh, was slouched in the second row.

When I slid next to him, Josh pressed his elbow into mine, scanned the mourners behind us, and whispered. "Where's Chuck?"

I nudged him back. "Working. Where's Holly?"

"Same. Hey, do we even know these people?"

I'd done my best to look sad up to that point, but a laugh slipped out, attracting the attention of an unfamiliar great-aunt who turned her entire body around for a conversation I'd hoped to avoid. She began to speak in a strange dialect that I couldn't decipher, so I nodded politely, silently praying the service would begin soon. Sensing my brother's stare, I stifled a giggle. The whole situation was pure lunacy, pretending that we were family to a woman practically a stranger to us, that we deeply mourned simply because she once bore the title *Mother*.

A man tapped on the microphone at the front of the room, indicating it was time for the service to begin. People hurried up to the coffin to tuck mementos around the deceased. With sad faces, they returned to their seats, nodding their condolences to Mom and her brothers as they passed by.

Finally, it was time for the immediate family to file past. "You don't have to," I whispered to the kids before I went to support Mom, who stood at the coffin in a trance-like state.

"Goodbye, Mother." She leaned down and placed her lips gently on Grandma's cold cheek, leaving a faint mark of red lipstick. Dad escorted Mom back to her seat, and I sat down before realizing I hadn't paused to pay my own respects. Did anyone notice? Did they already know how I felt? It wasn't hard to figure out that there was bad blood between Grandma and Mom. Mom's visits were more frequent once Grandma got sick, but I hadn't been here in years. Was Grandma even at my wedding? There may have been a disagreement days before. Something had been off with Grandma all my life, but no one had cared to explain.

The funeral director read the obituary, noting the time of birth and day of death, but not including much else other than naming family members departed before her and left behind. Then he looked at Mom. "Helen's daughter, Lynn, would like to say a few words."

This revelation would have shocked me into a resurrection had I been the body lying in the coffin. Mom? Speak? Mom rarely choked out a whole sentence in a private conversation, let alone in front of a roomful of people most likely wondering why she'd stayed away for so long.

I stared in disbelief as Mom stood and walked to the podium with her head held high. Who was this person? What would she say? Considering the possibilities, I tried not to squirm. *Oh no, this can't be good. It must be payback time, when the secret between mother and daughter will be revealed.*

Mom peeked at the paper in her hands, then looked up. Her eyes settled on me. *Dear Lord, what is she going to do up there?!*

She cleared her throat before she began. "The last time I saw my mother in the nursing home, she was very tired. She kept asking to be put to bed, but it was too early. To distract her, I took her for a walk around the hall in her wheelchair. When we were away from the nurse's station, I bent down and said to her, 'Mom, I know you love Jesus.'

"She said, 'I love Him, but I don't know if He loves me.'

"I reassured her. 'Oh yes, Mom; Jesus loves you; He really does.' " Would you please join me in singing the last song we sang together?"

The organist was unprepared for this unexpected program change, so Mom was forced to sing "Jesus Loves Me" a Capella. The notes broke and caught in places, but she trudged on. It was a daughter's sacrifice of love for a mother she loved but who she wasn't sure loved her.

Like a good daughter, I joined Mom so she wouldn't sing alone. Tears streamed down my face, but it wasn't for the grandma I hadn't known. I mourned for her daughter, who had tried to love her mother but didn't know if her effort was enough.

I cried because I knew all too well the feeling Mom expressed.

What you don't know *can* hurt you.

I learned that from her.

*   *   *

Dad and Mom volunteered to drive us home from the airport.

"It's silly for Chuck to drive all the way here when we're going right past your house," Dad argued. I couldn't refute his logic without revealing how I felt about spending one more hour with the woman slowly smothering me one heavy sigh at a time.

When they dropped us off in the driveway, I was at a breaking point. I stepped out of the car, wanting to run into the house like the kids. Instead, I dutifully stooped down. "Do you guys want to come in for a minute? Maybe go on a boat ride?" I hoped my invitation didn't sound too insincere, although it was. I couldn't wait to get back to my life. Mom's burst of love and bravery had ended the moment the casket closed.

Was she mad at me? It was highly possible. She'd walked up behind me as I filled Chuck in on the awkward funeral details by phone. Did she think I'd been laughing at her? Who knew? It was always something with her.

Dad smiled big, revealing silver-capped molars, suddenly unable to detect his grieving wife's mood. "OK, if you insist! Ha, ha!"

I hadn't insisted. But now I was in a pickle, suddenly remembering that Chuck had come home early for a quick family dinner before he had to return to the office.

Thankfully, Dad remembered his manners and turned to Mom. "Lynn? How about a boat ride?"

Mom looked down at her hands in her lap and flipped one over to check her cuticles. "I want to go home," she said.

As they drove off, a rush of guilt mixed with relief enveloped me. I decided to call and check on her mood later.

But I forgot. Two weeks passed and I hadn't checked on Mom. I had other things on my mind, like my marriage. "We're just two ships passing in the night," Chuck joked, hand in the air after reaching for mine as we passed in the hallway.

I hoisted the slipping laundry basket higher on my hip. "Oh, sorry. I thought you were grabbing a towel. Hold on. Let me put this down."

"Never mind. Gotta go." The door slammed. He was gone, headed back to work at the company he built from the ground up, the company he sold to buy us this lake house and where he was surrounded by beautiful, intelligent women who called him boss. I was sure that a few might want him to be more than that. Or at least they'd drop everything to grab his hand, unlike me, who was too distracted to be bothered.

I couldn't help but ruminate on the hallway encounter. Why was it so difficult to stop? Because I was under constant pressure to keep going and keep everything running: the dishwasher, the carpool, the washing machine, the grocery cart, the checkbook, the boat. Load 'em and unload 'em, no time to stop and think. If I failed as a mom, what good was I? But if I failed as a wife . . . I pushed that consequence from my mind. I could fix our relationship.

"Look at this beautiful lake!" I whined at dinner after Chuck announced he had to return to work. "You never want to have fun with just me. How about if you leave work early tomorrow, I send the kids to your sister's, and we row out to the middle of the lake and do nothing for *once* in our lives?"

My plea was a little dramatic, but I was desperate for results. If we were two ships passing, he was a speedboat; I was a canoe. Maybe a rowboat date would help us meet in the middle and bring romance into our crazy, busy lives.

The rowboat also had limited seating and would keep our date down to a party of two, which was crucial to my plan. The realtor had revealed the curse of lake living to me only after we signed the purchase agreement. "When you live on the lake, everyone shares a backyard." He was right. Our twenty-three foot deck boat attracted too much attention. Neighbors viewed an open seat as an invite to join the fun, and Chuck's motto was "the more the merrier." Since my motto was "less is more," I felt I had to make sure I was enough to keep him happy.

The next day, I had one foot out the door toward our date when the phone rang.

"C'mon!" Chuck urged. "Let's go. They'll leave a message!" His tone argued interruptions were much too common those days.

My earlier words blaming him for our lack of romance accused me, along with his eyes. But the way to marital reconciliation was blocked by the familiar number flashing on the answering machine. My heart dropped. "It's my mom."

Of course it was Mom. It was always Mom.

Mom was the ever-present force that pulled me close, churned my insides, and wrestled me to the ground while I scurried under the bed, barely escaping the emotional hairbrush that swatted inches from my tender bottom. "Wait till your father gets home, young lady," Mom threatened. But it's Mom who I was waiting to please. She held the real power, because if my own mother didn't love me, who could?

Mom preferred everything to be just so, but nothing about me ever felt up to her standards. One lingering look from her had me second-guessing my hair, clothes, words, and decisions. God forbid I chose wrong, because that meant I was all wrong. More than anything, I wanted to be all right. I wanted to be loved just as I was. After a while, I searched for someone to fill the vacancy she'd left.

It was too much to ask of anyone, but Chuck fit the bill when we married five days short of my twentieth birthday. Under his lovestruck gaze, I felt almost perfect. Maybe that's why I routinely called him mom throughout our honeymoon. The mistaken identity clouded our newlywed conversations and ruined any amorous notions. Much to my horror, it wasn't an easy habit to break. "Mom! I mean, Chuck." My face reddened at the subconscious label I applied to him repeatedly. Mom and Chuck were like night and day, but I needed them both to love me. Pleasing one meant disappointing the other. It was impossible to choose.

I stared at the answering machine, waiting and hoping for the kind of message other women received from their mothers or best friends, something like "Honey, I know you're busy, but I miss you! Let's go out and get our nails done. My treat." I would've given anything to hear "Nikki, you must call me immediately! I have the best piece of gossip about that nosy neighbor. You'll never believe who she's sleeping with."

After three more rings that felt like three hundred, the machine answered the call. "Nikki, it's your dad." His voice sounded thin and distant. "Please call me as soon as possible. Your mom and I need to talk to you. It's important."

Good Lord, what did I do NOW? Panic shot through my mind like a pinball, bouncing off one conversation to another while I kept the flippers moving until I could find the reason that led to this summons. Turning up nothing, I punched my arms into my coat. *I'll be damned if one more worry about her keeps me from enjoying my life.* "I'll call them later." I shoved all scenarios of doom to the back of my mind and shut the door behind me.

I scanned the horizon for any more obstacles and noticed the edge of the sky, bright blue moments before, had become tinged with ominous gray. "Are those thunderclouds?" I asked, disappointed in myself. I should have moved quicker, should have checked the weather. When the phone rang, I should have run down the hill, jumped in the rowboat, and said, "Who the heck cares? I'm allowed to have some fun!"

Instead, I'd been paralyzed. Caught between pleasing myself

and honoring my mother, I'd managed to do neither.

I regained my composure by stooping to retie my laces while Chuck readied the boat. For a moment, it was merely another ordinary day in the life of a woman used to being lost in a sea of regrets. "Woulda, coulda, shoulda," I muttered, wrestling to push the shame away. Why did I care what she thought? I was a thirty-six-year-old woman! *I will not cry. I will not cry.* I was fighting a battle I'd never come close to winning.

But I was soon to discover that things are not always what they seem. In the midst of ordinary life, an extraordinary thought slipped into my mind. It wasn't a normal, everyday, fleeting thought. It seemed spoken by another, in a way that felt weighty and settled in my chest right next to my breaking heart. Without question, I knew the thought came from God, though I wasn't sure I'd ever heard His voice before.

Hearing from the Creator troubled me. Throughout my childhood, I was mesmerized by the variety of Bible characters that trekked across the flannelgraph in Sunday School. Adam, Abraham, Moses, and Mary were all qualified to hear God speak. Me? I was always falling short, one verse shy of receiving the highest award, one good deed away from being who God wanted me to be. Just as I shied from Mom's examination, I didn't want God looking too close.

But God had said, *Yea, though I walk through the valley of the shadow of death, I will fear no evil.*[3] I second-guessed the cryptic message, dismissing it as requiring further decoding down the road. *Mom can't be THAT mad at me, can she?*

I said nothing about the message to Chuck, fearing he'd assume I was turning out like my mother after all, practically speaking in tongues. While the boat pushed off, I steadied myself by gripping

---

[3] Psalm 23:4a (KJV).

the cold metal sides, determined to put God's voice behind me and enjoy the adventure ahead. The wind picked up, causing the waves to slap the side of the boat and rock it with the steady rhythm of a mother lovingly rocking her child.

Water splashed my feet as I recalled the last part of the verse. Apparently, God wasn't finished talking. There was more He wanted to say. *For thou art with me.*[4] I put two and two together, piecing together the message. *Though I walk through the valley of the shadow of death, I will fear no evil, for You are with me.* Maybe that verse had been read at Grandma's funeral?

Good grief, yes! That made sense. Here I was thinking it was more than it was, Heaven's secret message. But it was only a Bible verse, one I knew by heart.

Chuck appeared lost in his thoughts while I was busy interpreting God's. Neither of us jumped when the lightning slashed the sky.

---

[4] Psalm 23:4b (KJV).

Chapter 2

Cut Off

We pulled anchor when the horizon tinged green and static lifted our hair. Was that a siren wailing in the distance? Only a tornado could force me back inside to face the storm that I suspected brewed on the answering machine.

After we docked the boat, we tried to outrun the rain, taking the steep steps from the lake to the house two at a time. Before we reached the door, fate poured over us in buckets. Most days, I'd have thrown my head back and cackled at the sky, amused at the ridiculous notion that I could outmaneuver the inevitable. I preferred to laugh instead of cry. But by the sound of Dad's voice earlier, I assumed laughter wasn't appropriate.

I stomped soaking wet feet on the door mat and involuntarily shivered before resolutely reaching for the phone. My finger felt heavy as I punched in my old number from my parents' home. *Might as well get this over with.*

Dad answered on the first ring, like a lion waiting to pounce and dutifully drag me before the lioness. "Your mom and I need to talk to you. We want to come over." His tone meant business.

"Come over? Now?" This must be worse than I thought. I

glanced at Chuck. This date was a disaster. "Sorry, Dad. I'm busy right now. Can you tell me what you need to over the phone?" I looked at my watch. There was still time for a movie before the kids were due back. At this point, a comedy sounded nice.

"No."

What on earth had I done? Dad never told me no.

Then I heard her voice in the background, low and frantic, directing her husband on what to say. Whatever the offense, it must be a doozy for Dad to abandon diplomacy.

"Dad? Tell me now, please." I hated sounding like my five-year-old self, every ounce of me leaning the opposite way as Daddy pulled me across the elementary school lobby. My heels dug in and drew a line across the freshly waxed linoleum right up to my assigned seat in the kindergarten classroom. Two weeks of school taught me all I needed to know. I wanted to stay home with Mommy and my new little brother. But Daddy said I was a big girl now.

Why did his silence over the phone unnerve me? The whispered discussion started up again. I couldn't quite make out what my parents were saying to each other, but it wasn't good. Shouldn't this part of my life be settled by now? My hands shouldn't be so shaky. At what point does love that has felt conditional give its final answer so you can stop second-guessing it? I was a grown woman with two children of her own. Why was I being treated like a child? Why did they drive me to act like one?

"Dad!?" Through gritted teeth, I commanded his attention. "Tell me now!" I wanted to get it over with, move forward, and enjoy my one wonderful life as best I could. If it had to be without achieving my endless quest for my mother's approval for some reason, so be it.

The sideline conversation continued as if no one heard my outburst. Dad spoke in the soothing language of a skilled caretaker.

"Lynn, we have to tell her."

Tell me what? The floor creaked as Chuck moved closer to hear. I squeezed my eyes shut, pressed the receiver against my ear, and waited for the verdict.

"Mom's had a rash for a while." I was speechless. This whole roller-coaster ride had nothing to do with me? I reached back in time to connect this new bit of information to something old. When she'd grabbed at her bag as we were boarding the plane, her scarf had slipped, revealing an angry red streak running down her neck. I thought the revelation strange. First, she never wore scarves. Second, her olive skin was normally flawless.

One mystery solved.

Dad was a man of many words, so I bit my tongue and let him ramble, relieved at the news. Something was wrong, but a rash was a relatively simple dilemma. They needed my help to solve a problem. Why all the drama? The tension left my shoulders. *Silly me.* Maybe I was the drama queen, not her.

"A rash, huh? Hmmm." Did she buy a new detergent? Get talked into a new shampoo? "Can I talk to Mom? I'm wondering if—"

"Nikki . . ."

"Yeah, Dad?" More silence. I didn't have time for this. "Hey, Dad? Can I call you back?"

Chuck had wandered away into the next room; I heard the strum of a guitar. I was losing him.

But I wasn't prepared for the magnitude of loss that came with Dad's next revelation.

"Your mom has breast cancer."

My soul was severed from its body, the guillotine sharpened by those five words. My dream for me and Mom to become forever best friends dropped into a bloody basket and stared back, lifeless.

"Wh-what? What'd you say?" I sat down hard on the landing, too dizzy to take in the details, unable to believe it was true. For all the canyons that laid between Mom and me, I had never imagined a grave. Not so soon.

This wasn't the way life worked. If you do what God says, you receive blessings, not curses. Though Mom and I had some contentious moments, Mom believed in Jesus more than anyone I knew. He wouldn't let her die.

The car keys hung by the front door. I didn't look back, because I couldn't explain. There was no time to waste. I needed to get to Mom before anything else got in the way.

With a turn of the ignition, "Highway to Hell", the AC/DC song that was my high school anthem, screamed through the speakers. Without thinking, I shut the devil down and drove.

The sudden storm had passed, leaving gulleys along the street like the thoughts that streamed through my head. What would I tell the kids? Was Mom going to die? Did she know how much I loved her?

I wove through the streets at breakneck speeds. Mom wasn't quite five miles away but felt unreachable. Every year, she felt farther and farther away. How often had I made this trip, unsure of her reaction to my arrival? Most times, her face fell when our eyes met, as if she was expecting someone else, a daughter who was more like her and easier to love.

I did my best to make up for all my wild teenage years, though she never knew the sum of them. Sometimes, I think she suspected her little girl hadn't grown up to be an angel after all. Rather than call me out, she employed ruthless tactics I was sure were meant to manipulate me into changing. Like she did after I spent the eve of my nineteenth birthday slamming kamikazes in a bar's bathroom stall. The next morning, a birthday poem she penned for me waited on the kitchen table.

You're such a special blessing sent from
God above. You're joy and peace and
everything that we were dreaming of.

Thankfully, I made it to the bathroom before I threw up. Full of neither joy nor peace, I didn't want to be constrained by my parents' dreams. I had dreams of my own.

Following in Mom's footsteps, though, I married my Prince Charming. Later, I overheard Mom tell her friends that my rebellious years began when I became an adult, as if she declared me a rebel anew with each independent step I took. Eventually, I'd decide it was only fair that I give her a new label, too.

* * *

"Mom's a BITCH! Do you hear me, Dad? She's a BIIIIIIIIIIITCH!" I rolled down the car window and spit the words out at him in a blood-curdling scream that brought curious looks from the neighbors.

I meant to hurt her, not embarrass him, but Dad's face told me I'd hit the wrong target. Neither he nor I knew what we'd done to incur such wrath from a person who was supposed to love us.

"Go!" I gave Chuck the green light to leave my parents' driveway before I changed my mind. He pressed the gas, and our car's bald tires spun in reverse, spraying gravel into the freshly mown yard.

I should have seen it coming. We were newly married, in between apartments, needing a temporary place to stay for a month. I thought Mom would welcome me back with open arms. Instead, she'd crossed them and pressed her lips in a firm, thin line.

I'd smiled brightly, ignoring the rejection, too embarrassed to acknowledge that my mother wasn't happy to see me as I descended into her basement with laundry baskets of shoes and my old sleeping bag from church camp. I apologized profusely for the intrusion, telling her we wouldn't make a peep, and then profusely to my new husband for being the daughter of a woman who hated him without a cause.

"I don't get it," Chuck would muse under the covers. "All the moms of the other girls I dated always loved me."

I tried not to think about all the girls he'd dated, because they and their mothers probably looked pretty good then compared to me and my mom. I couldn't figure out why Mom didn't like Chuck. He was charming, polite, successful, and willing to yield should Mom take the slightest offense. His only fault may have been his honesty based on their very first conversation when he came to pick me up for a date.

"Chuck, your face is a little red? Do you have a sunburn?"

"No, Lynn. I had a few beers with clients."

Knowing this openness couldn't continue, I attempted to help Chuck navigate the murky waters at the next family dinner by gently tapping him with my foot when he was heading out of bounds. That didn't work either. "Nikki, why are you kicking me?" Perhaps the real problem was that Chuck couldn't be controlled.

Before we drifted off to sleep the first night of our stay in my parents' home, we concluded that Mom would have preferred I marry the pastor's son. I didn't mention my brief affair with the church bad boy. Deep down, I wanted a hero who could lead me out of the carefully constructed house of cards I grew up in. I longed for a place to keep my shoes on and not be afraid to step on toes.

Each night, I set the alarm for an ungodly hour so we could take turns tiptoeing up two flights of stairs to shower in the only bathroom before dawn. I let Chuck go first so I could follow to wipe down the sink, gather the wet towels, and replace them with a fresh set. If I used a coffee cup, it was washed, wiped, and put away before Mom's slippered feet descended the stairs. Our entire meager budget was quickly consumed by eating out every morning and night, then driving around the block until our gas tank dipped to empty and the porch light came on. Regardless of our efforts to avoid Mom, staying with my parents was a disaster waiting to happen.

Every family has its own version of normal. Growing up, my normal sifted through two filters, Mom's current mood and the Holy Scriptures. Chuck's mode of operation fell somewhere between dodging Dad's beer cans and employing good old common sense. Those two "normals" struggled to coexist. It was amazing our stay with my parents lasted a week.

On the Saturday afternoon we finally left, Chuck and I had bravely emerged from the basement and perched on the sofa in the living room. Tension had filled the air since morning, when I'd overheard my parents discussing my sixteen-year-old brother's curfew violation.

"Warren, I think you're being too hard on Josh." While Dad held his ground, pans banged, water sloshed, and Mom aggressively washed dishes.

"Mom, can I help you?" I called out, but I knew the answer before her clipped response.

"I'm fine."

Chuck and I exchanged a glance. Three more weeks to go.

Overhead, my brother stomped back and forth in his room, shaking the walls in protest of his punishment. Eventually, the noise stopped, as if he was contemplating his next move.

"Warren?" Mom appeared, her ear cocked toward the ceiling. Dad had fled the scene. "Joshua?" she called out next, focusing on the spot above where her second-born endured his torture. She was greeted with crickets.

Clearly, my brother was playing possum, the oldest trick in the book. But I suspected it never crossed Mom's mind that her favorite child could manipulate the situation. To her, his silence signaled danger.

In desperation, Mom turned to my husband. "Chuck? What should I do?" She was a damsel in distress, and my husband was a problem solver.

My eyes darted to the nearest Bible on the coffee table. Picking that up would've been a good move, but Chuck reacted on pure instinct. "Why don't you listen to Warren," he suggested, "and let Josh figure it out on his own?" Chuck had a little brother, too, but no one handled the two of them with kid gloves. Instead, Chuck's dad gave them boxing gloves and threw them into the ring.

Mom's face went white, then beet red as she processed that advice. The fate of her one and only son would not be left to chance. Didn't this outsider know that Josh had been dedicated to the Lord?

"Chuck White!" she screamed, pure hatred in her eyes. "I'm sick and tired of your judgments and criticisms!"

Judgments? Criticisms? I racked my brain for evidence to support the accusation but found none. Actually, Chuck's behavior around my mother was the opposite.

"You look lovely, Lynn!" he'd say at every opportunity. "Lynn, what do you think?" he'd ask. He complimented her with "This is the best spaghetti I've ever had!"

Much to my holy horror, I'd once witnessed Mom and her prayer buddies dancing around my good-natured fiancé, waving their hankies and speaking in tongues. I was mortified, but Chuck assured me that he appreciated their prayers.

Now under maternal duress, Mom was no longer filled with the Spirit; she was filled to the brim with the devil's fury. She stomped up the stairs, her neck lined with popped vessels, while Chuck stood dazed and condemned. He had displeased the queen.

I couldn't believe that I'd been so foolish. Why had I expected

Mom to embrace my new husband when she never fully accepted me? Something inside me snapped.

"You're a BITCH!!!" I screamed it at the top of my lungs, forcing all the hurt I'd swallowed to the surface, pounding each syllable through the floorboards so my rage would shake her. "You're a BITCH!!" I shouted again. Once my pent-up feelings were out, I couldn't stop the words from erupting through angry sobs again and again. I'd held my tongue for so long.

There was no reply from the second-story bedrooms. Though two humans were housed there, not a creaking floorboard or heavy sigh emerged as the dust of my tantrum settled. I didn't hear if my brother's door opened a crack. There was no indication from the next bedroom over that Mom heard or cared what I thought.

In one decisive move, I redirected my anger and descended into the basement in a frenzy of grief, scooping up blankets, throwing hangers and shoes back into the laundry basket, and making myself disappear from my parents' home. Every sign that I existed was hauled out to our car in fifteen minutes flat. Hopes, dreams, and tears spilled out onto the green shag carpet of my childhood, and I didn't bother tidying up after myself.

Grasping the handle of the side door, I paused to turn and take one last look across the kitchen counter where, for most of my life, Mom had lovingly set breakfast down before me on a brown floral plate every single morning. Beyond that counter sat the antique oak table our little family of four encircled at dinner each evening, heads bowed, hands squeezed, the scene punctuated with a hearty amen, like the good Christian family everyone thought we were. What a bunch of hypocrites.

To make sure she knew I was leaving for good, I pulled the aluminum storm door shut so hard the glass rattled. Dad heard the commotion and came running from the neighbor's yard, where he might have been enjoying a nice little chat about the joys of a soon-to-be-empty nest and how quickly children grow up and fly away. Not fully discerning the magnitude of the situation, he pleaded with us to stay, but the damage had been done.

Later, I assumed he'd find her swollen-eyed and sullen, buried under the heavy blanket of regret. She'd be declared the victim, a delicate flower trampled down by a careless, wayward child. My version of the story wouldn't matter.

There was no turning back. Chuck leaned forward over the steering wheel, gaining speed and distance on a road filled with potholes. As we fishtailed over the hill, I looked in the rearview mirror. Wait, was I seeing things? Did her bedroom curtains move? Why did I keep hoping that things would get better? It hurt too much. I forced my gaze ahead and vowed to never look back.

But love doesn't work that way.

* * *

Over the years, I never overcame the guilt of my outburst the day Chuck and I left my parents' home. Sure, the hard feelings had softened over time. Mom and I eventually hugged, but when we did, it felt like there was less of her left for me to try to love.

Racing toward her side at the news of cancer, I wondered how long I'd pay for the sin of being human. Whatever it took, I was ready to pay my debt. I wanted the stamp of approval that declared me paid in full, not return to sender. I wanted my mom to tell her friends what a "good daughter" I was.

Maybe this cancer scare could be a new beginning. As I traveled back over the same hill I'd used to escape from her, my heart beat faster, then quickly sunk to the pit of my stomach. I was too late. She'd already called in reinforcements, because she needed them more than she needed me. Or maybe she never expected me to show up at all.

I hit the brakes to keep a safe distance from the people who could hurt me, realizing that my mother was one of them. Caution was necessary.

I'd learned that from her.

Chapter 3

Heart Problems

A blue sedan and maroon minivan were parked haphazardly in the driveway. The prayer wagons had already circled. I didn't have to go inside to know what was happening. Bottles of anointing oil were cracked open, prayer cloths were waving, and cancer demons were commanded to flee—all in Jesus's name, of course.

Good. I hoped God heard her friends' prayers, because my prayers weren't up to their level. I had never qualified as holy enough to receive the "signs that followed those that believed."[5] I believed, but apparently less than I should, or I'd have my own heavenly prayer language by now to petition God for Mom's healing.

Once I got my nerve up, I released the brake and inched past the house slowly once, twice, a third time, hoping that someone inside would open their eyes for a moment and notice Lynn's daughter had arrived and that, perhaps, this was a private family matter. Of course the word "family" expanded once you entered the family of God.

---

[5] Mark 16:17 (KJV).

Upon entry, the adult titles of "Mr" and "Mrs" were replaced with "Brother" and "Sister," which carried more privileges and responsibilities. As a church family, we were supposed to "bear each other's burdens" and "lay down our lives" yet I hadn't stuck around long enough to earn the title "Sister". I'm sure as far as they were concerned, I was still a child, not quite ready to bear Mom's new burden since I was a bit of a burden myself.

I kept circling the block, hitting the same pothole over and over again. Damn the stupid street! When would it be fixed once and for all? I was almost out of gas before I realized I couldn't do it. I couldn't pretend to be part of the holy roller gang. That I attended a church where people rarely raised their hands had caused Mom concern. "Is it Spirit-filled?" she asked, biting her bottom lip to refrain from further comment. Her lack of enthusiasm over my choice of church told me how she really felt. I was close to acceptable, almost, but not quite.

My shortfall was a pity, because Mom practically birthed me between the pews. But the bar was set too high from the start.

* * *

In 1968, four-year-old Sunday School girls like me were put on the fast track to holy living. Through keen observation, I learned that a good girl should be seen and not heard, so I thoughtfully considered the scuffs on my Mary Jane shoes, waiting for Mommy to conclude her after-church conversation with her "sisters."

"You look lovely today, Nicole," said Sister Baker. "Did your Mommy make your dress?"

I looked up, startled at being addressed during an adult conversation. Mommy smiled and nodded, giving me her permission to tell the truth. I dipped my head, nervously swishing the fabric of my skirt back and forth.

The sisters oohed and aahed at Mommy's handiwork; I

squirmed while Mommy blushed. Receiving a compliment felt sinful, though Mommy spent hours getting me ready for the Lord. Presenting your family to the Lord without spot or wrinkle was a Christian mother's duty that she took very seriously. I had no choice in the matter.

Preparations began on Saturday evening since Sunday was the Sabbath. Mommy spent the afternoon pressing our best Sunday clothes until they were crisp. Daddy polished the family footwear with an old t-shirt and petroleum jelly. I worked on lingering in the tub until my fingers and toes were pruned and the water tepid, knowing the next dreaded step in the beauty process.

Despite my loud protests, Mommy quietly combed through my wet snarls, careful not to tug too hard, but pain was inevitable on the road to holy living. I looked for every opportunity to bolt up the stairs and hide in my closet like the reluctant saint-in-training I was. Mommy had to use her knees as a vise on my shoulders to complete the holy work of setting my freshly combed hair into pink sponge curlers, which made a good night's sleep next to impossible.

I woke up Sunday morning looking forward to the free time between morning and evening church services when I was released from my Christian duties of being beautiful and good and allowed to take a nap in my slip and tights. Taking off all that constraining finery felt more like Heaven to me.

"I hear someone has a birthday coming up?"

Before I realized I was being asked another question, Mommy answered for me. "Yes! Nicole was born on Mother's Day. She waited for the church service to be over before she arrived. Wasn't that sweet of her?" Their pleased reactions followed me throughout my life. I couldn't escape the feeling that since I had so much control of my first birth, I'd also be in charge of my second birth.

Every Sunday School girl knew that second births happen at the church altar, soon followed by the best birthday gift of all, receiving your very own heavenly language so that you could talk to God, proof that you were both seen and heard. It was a glorious and lofty idea for little old me.

Mommy didn't grow up in church like I did, but somewhere along the way, she found Jesus and received this special gift. The two of them had frequent conversations that I couldn't decipher, but through her tears and groans, I understood she was begging Him for a miracle that wasn't happening.

From where I sat, it was hard to process delays in God's responses. I was born into a world where people were pushed down front in a wheelchair, healed instantly, and returned to their seats, leaping and dancing a jig. Ushers kept tape measures in the pockets of their suit coats to verify limb-growing miracles. Sisters waited in the wings with blankets for those lucky enough to be slain in the Spirit. It didn't seem fair that Mommy was overlooked.

One summer Monday, I woke up to discover my Sunday dress hanging on my bedroom door. Before I could run down the stairs to report the error, Mommy announced we'd be going to revival service every night that week. After dinner, I climbed into our car's back seat, envious of the neighborhood kids hauling balls and bats out to play. I reminded myself that sinners might look like they were having more fun, but Heaven would be worth the required church time.

The August air barely moved through the sanctuary, but the evangelist said that God was among us. One by one, the old and young quietly slipped into the aisle to make their way down to meet Him while the choir sang "Just As I Am." The evangelist whispered that Jesus was silently calling, pulling at people's hearts. Jesus must have touched mine. Without a word to Mommy, I joined the stream of sinners coming to the altar to be washed in the blood.

It was standing room only at the foot of the cross. Solemnly, the evangelist bowed his head over the microphone in his hand and led us in the sinners' prayer. I bowed my head, closed my eyes, and repeated the prayer word for word. I wanted to be born again and knew it needed to be done right.

When I opened my eyes, the minister held the microphone out to me and asked the most important question I'd ever been asked. "Where is Jesus now?" The congregation leaned forward in smiling anticipation, and I stared down into the little holes that covered the mouthpiece. Which one should I speak to? There were so many to choose from, like there were so many places Jesus could be at the moment. I knew the answer; Jesus was in my heart. But glancing around at all those earnest faces led me to believe they expected me to deliver a bigger story.

"I think He's playing baseball?" I replied. The loud laughter startled me, filling me with shame. Mommy appeared, took my hand, and walked me past curious onlookers craning their necks to see the girl who didn't have the correct answer. We ducked our heads and focused on our feet until we reached the parking lot.

My shame was her shame, too. A Christian mother's job was to not only present her daughter to the Lord, but to also teach her His ways. More trips to the altar were in our future, and Mommy and Jesus had their work cut out for them.

* * *

The needle on the gas gauge hovered over *E*. I was running out of patience as well. I'd have to return home if Mom's friends didn't leave soon. I hated to be a quitter when the stakes were so high.

Why was I so afraid to face them? They were nice enough people. Their only fault was that they thought they were holier than me. In their pious opinion, I wasn't saved. I didn't argue. Instead, I avoided them, because I was afraid they were right.

* * *

I should never have signed us up for the Young Married Bible Study, but it felt important to begin my marriage on the right foot. Pushing aside my qualms about being trapped in a tiny, enclosed room with so many sets of curious eyes, I marched in toting the brand-new NIV Bible Mom had given us as a wedding gift. In the event any doubt remained, I positioned the black leather book on my lap so anyone nearby could read the custom gold engraving. *Charles and Nicole White. Any questions, ladies?*

Jack led the study. He had a loud, commanding way about him that made me skittish. He stood at the front and held his Bible in one hand while he swept the room with the other. Each time his hand passed over, it seemed to be pointing at me. I slumped in my chair, leaned over my Bible, and pretended to be extra interested in a verse. "Let's go around the room and give our testimonies," he suggested. "Let everyone get to know each other."

My heart started to pound, and my back broke into sweat. I didn't have a testimony, not really. I had no epiphany when Heaven opened, no precise moment that magically transformed me from sinner to saint. Salvation surely "took" at some point, but I traveled back and forth to the altar so many times to rededicate myself to the Lord that I lost track of when it happened. How many times was a person allowed to lose their salvation and find it again? That was a question I didn't dare ask.

Thankfully, Jack began the introductions at the other side of the room. One by one, the stories came out. A smartly dressed businesswoman had poured her hidden whiskey bottles down the drain in one decisive moment, and a weeping blonde's life was changed at age sixteen, when she answered an altar call at church camp. A gray-templed man stood and cleared his throat, saying only "March 27, 1963," then sitting back down.

Even my new husband had a salvation story I knew by heart. "A Baptist bus used to stop by my house every Sunday when I was nine years old. I was always too busy playing to go to church, but my older sister, Debbie, went. One week, all the children on the bus were promised a Slo Poke sucker if they brought a friend with them the following Sunday, so she convinced me to go." Cue the laughter. It happened every time. "I sat in the church basement, and a man told me that Jesus had died on the cross for my sins, then rose again. I believed that, and well, here I am."

There was so much more to his story—how Jesus gave hope to a little boy who lived in a world of empty bottles, bruising words, and pillows that couldn't block out the sound of his mother crying. But Chuck sensed that testimony time was short, and Jack wanted everyone to have a turn. With my husband's salvation verified, all eyes were on me.

"Nikki, how about you?" Jack asked, his shadow falling over me as I shifted. "When were you saved?"

Any time I was questioned about my faith, my body had the same reaction. My breathing became shallow, and heat from my chest rose past my neck to color my cheeks crimson. Since the beginning, my salvation story never held up to scrutiny.

"Um, I went to the altar and gave my heart to Jesus when I was little. I don't know exactly how old I was. Four? No, probably five. It's been so long, I can't remember the exact date." I swallowed hard, reached for the Coke I'd set on the floor, and took a sip. Then I set it back down hoping no one noticed my hands shook.

You don't know the date?" Jack questioned, eyebrows raised, beady eyes staring through me.

My head bobbled to neither confirm nor deny. I'd been trained to believe that someone other than me would have to decide such an important matter.

"If you don't know the date or remember the moment, then you aren't saved." His deep voice resounded like a judge's gavel, driving a stake through my heart.

The fear I lugged back and forth to church each Sunday sunk into the pit of my stomach. I'd known it was true from the fateful moment I couldn't answer the minister's question about where Jesus was. I was a fraud, imposter, heretic—a hypocrite who didn't belong in His church. It all made sense now why I heard crickets every time I asked God for the gift of speaking in tongues.

"Jesus, Jesus, Jesus." With each request, I'd chant His name like a magic word, begging Him to notice, forgive, and help me be better. The elders took pity on me, laying their hands on my shoulders and back, pushing me off balance with their passion for the Lord. Did they hope I'd topple over from their efforts and finally be filled with the Holy Spirit? Eventually, they'd wander off in search of another seeker with a little more faith, and I'd slink away hating myself, wondering if I'd ever be sinless enough to receive God's stamp of approval.

Jack's harsh judgment of me during the Bible study finally left no room for discussion. I quickly gathered my things, and Chuck escorted me through the pitiful looks of God's chosen. I broke away, walking faster and faster down the hall toward the silent, dimly lit sanctuary, staring down at the carpet, the white-painted cinder-block walls of my childhood closing in.

I paused briefly at the entrance and took it all in, like I had done on my wedding day a few months before, when the room was full of life and possibility. Now, it felt stark and empty—the pews, the pulpit, even the cross. The altar taunted me to return and ask God for one more sign that He wasn't finished with me yet.

But another sign caught my eye: blood-red letters splattered across white paint pure as driven snow. EXIT. As I stepped closer, the silver bar on the door gave a warning. *Emergency Exit Only.*

I pushed hard against all the unasked questions and unsatisfying answers, daring the alarm to sound. I didn't care. Let them come and get me. Then I'd tell them what I really thought of their silly set of impossible rules.

The door swung wide open without a sound, as if God no longer cared. I stepped out into the parking lot, where one car waited with its engine idling. Chuck sat behind the wheel, the only savior I had left.

* * *

My ancient memory of exiting the church I'd grown up attending stung as I drove past Mom's house one last time, hoping that God had cleared His people out of my way. I couldn't seem to see past them.

Their cars hadn't moved. So, like the good girl Mommy wanted me to be, I decided not to disrupt their healing service. It was late. She was probably exhausted; I certainly was. Whatever needed to be said could wait until tomorrow. In the meantime, I'd hate myself for being a coward.

I'd learned that from her.

Chapter 4

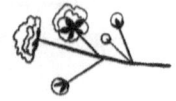

Full Circle

My car knew the way home and practically drove itself. Thank God, because I could barely navigate the circumstances, let alone the roads that wound around the many Michigan lakes in our area. It's funny how people end up where they do. Chuck and I seemed to bounce from house to house, unaware that each move brought us closer to our roots. I'd been so optimistic that our first house would be our last.

Two years after I left Mom's and God's houses, we put a down payment on a charming brick bungalow miles away from the neighborhood I'd known. I'd barely unpacked when I saw something I thought might be my wild imagination, so I asked Chuck to weigh in. He looked over my shoulder at the plastic stick I held up to the morning light.

"Is that a pink line?" I asked, pulling it closer for inspection.

Chuck's shout almost launched me from the bed. "A baby! We're gonna have a baby!" His reaction shouldn't have surprised me, but it did. Chuck was born to turn on a dime. I needed a minute.

Outside the window, a tree branch seemed to wiggle its

diamond-shaped leaves like delicate fingers. Fluffy clouds floated by. For the first time in years, my nose caught the scent of a familiar blossom that faithfully bloomed late each year. I inhaled the fragrance of new beginnings but resisted the urge to run out and gather a bouquet.

There was so much to do, and it was hard to know where to start. If I was going to be a mother, it was time to put aside childish things and get to work. My perception was that an adult did everything right, so I set out to do just that for the next eight months. But I was terrified of what would happen after the crib was delivered and set up and all the teensy outfits were hung in the closet.

I only had to wait two days past my due date to find out.

* * *

"It's a girl!" The doctor's announcement was the biggest surprise of my life. I was so sure my baby was a boy. My thoughts boomeranged from Tonka trucks to prom dresses, finally landing on a wedding gown.

Instinctively, I prepared my heart to lose her before I even held her in my arms. What's wrong with me? It stemmed back to Mom. How could I be a good mother if I was a bad daughter? But there was no time left to worry.

"Are you ready?" the nurse asked. Would I ever be? My arms felt as if they were made of rubber, but power surged through my veins at the sight of my daughter.

Most new mommas unwrap their babies to count each finger and toe. But who my girl was inside mattered more to me. To truly behold her, I had to stare into her eyes, the windows of her soul.

"Hello, Kati Girl." Her inky blue eyes met my gaze, and we considered each other, mother to daughter, and daughter to mother. When the cord connecting us was severed with a quick snip, I prayed a greater one would hold fast.

The nurse stood nearby, waiting to take my baby so the doctor could repair damage done to my body. But it was my daughter's wholeness I was worried about. Would she be OK without me? I never wanted to let her go. Whatever the sacrifice, she was worth it.

As if she felt the same way, Kati protested with a little cry, and I broke protocol. She needed to know that I would always love her, no matter what came between us. I pulled her close, quickly unwrapping her and me and all the layers between us. *I'm all yours, precious girl. That is, if you'll have me.* In a heartbeat, she was my world, and I was hers. In another beat, it felt like something was missing.

Fear sidled up with a finger on its chin, considering my qualifications. *Hmm, are you sure you have enough?* The day before, I'd have given the same old no answer, but a yes had been born.

I reached down into the deepest part of me and drew from the well of love within. Like pulling a rope with one hand leap-frogging another, I strained against the weight of a joy I didn't deserve. I'd risk facing every drop of doubt for my child so she wouldn't know hunger. Whatever I had left was hers for the taking. Yes, yes, a lifetime of yes, little girl. Was that how all mothers felt?

Mothers! I hadn't called Mom yet. Now that I'd accomplished this long-awaited feat, I felt sheepish about refusing her entry to the once-in-a-lifetime event. Was it selfish to want to keep it between my husband and me? I looked at Chuck, who hovered over the two of us, equally smitten.

"She's something, isn't she?" I asked.

"So are you." He gently pushed the hair away from my swollen eyes.

I shook off the compliment. I could never take the credit. This child was a work of art—God's work, not mine.

"I should call Mom." I appreciated that she'd played by my rules. To her credit, twenty-four hours had passed since she'd heard from me, and she hadn't charged up to the hospital. After an hour of motherhood, I considered her restraint with the utmost respect. The first-time grandma had nerves of steel.

Chuck dialed the phone, checking the clock on the wall. It was late, after ten, but this news could no longer wait. "Lynn? Hi! Yes, yes. Everything's fine. It's a GIRL! . . . Nikki? Yes, she's great . . . OK, hold on. I'll let you talk to her. It might be a stretch."

I laughed at the irony. Chuck wasn't kidding. The new beginning I'd longed for remained out of reach until Mom and I connected. Chuck walked the receiver toward the bed as far as he could, but the taut cord fell short of my outstretched hand. Undeterred, he made up the difference with one quick tug, tearing the phone out of the wall. It dangled by frayed wires, ending all hope of a once-in-a-lifetime reconnection with the one woman I was meant to share it with.

Time stood still as Chuck and I reflected on the enormity of the situation. *Lord, I hope that's not a sign of things to come.* I'd have to wait and trust that this baby could work her magic between her grandmother and me. Why couldn't she? Kati was a wonder to behold.

And as it happened, Mom and I agreed for the first time ever.

* * *

"She likes to keep moving, I think," I told Mom on the phone, moving the stroller back and forth in the kitchen.

"Sounds like someone I know," Mom replied.

Mom and I were living in a season of grace, so I tried hard not to take offense at what appeared to be backhanded compliments. Her keen observation was spot on. I was told that once I could stand alone, I wriggled out of my mother's arms and made her chase me. The delightful game for me wore her out. I could only pray that I'd have the strength to never let Kati get away. Thankfully, I was young and up to the challenge.

On a rough day when our home's walls seemed to be closing in on me and I mused about my chances of qualifying for sainthood, I impatiently threaded Kati's wriggling fingers through the arms of her jean jacket. Neither of us liked feeling stuck. A walk would do us both some good.

It was a perfect day, and like our charmed life, the stroller whizzed down the sidewalk, surprising sparrows that rested in a hydrangea bush. I stopped to watch as they fluttered to the next refuge. Becoming a mother made me see the world through Kati's eyes, which sometimes made me a little nervous. She was so full of questions.

"Momma?"

"Hmmm?"

"Where'd the birdies go?"

I launched into an explanation of migration, much too complicated for a two-year-old, let alone her twenty-four-year-old mother, who began to hope the neighbors' windows weren't open. I sounded ridiculous, giving anyone within earshot reason to believe that daycare was a much better educational option.

Kati's next line of inquiry interrupted my explanation and seemed to come out of nowhere. "Momma? Where's God?"

Where's God? The question that stumped me years ago flew up at me and perched on my shoulder. The most important questions always return, demanding answers until the ring of a bell signals you've answered right.

Where is God? All the possible responses ran through my head. *He's up in Heaven. He's with us. He's all around us.* But how did you explain that to a toddler? Of course, there was the most important answer. *He's in your heart.* Trying to explain that concept would lead to more questions I wasn't qualified to answer. We needed a little backup here, and I hadn't set foot in a church since that day I ran out the emergency exit.

Later that night, I reported the incident to Chuck. "Your mom probably put her up to it," he concluded.

I agreed with his theory. Where'd this curiosity about God come from? Most likely, Mom had something to do with it.

Looking back, it made sense. She'd been eager to babysit, even at the drop of a hat. No sooner did I pick up the phone than she was in our driveway. Secretly, I admired her stealth moves to point her grandchild in the proper direction. It wasn't wrong. Every child needed to learn about God. Merely singing "Jesus Loves Me" every night wouldn't cut it beyond a certain age. Mom had more wisdom than to come right out and say that. Instead, she slipped the message into Kati's thought pocket for me to find.

Finding an acceptable church would prove to be a challenge. Not only would it have to be affirmed by Mom, who'd recently fled from our former church to another, more charismatic fellowship, but Chuck had to be comfortable, too. My husband's hand still stung from a slap he received as a boy when he reached for the communion plate in error. "You're not a member," his grandma hissed. I didn't want to be one of those wives who attended church with her kids and left her husband home watching the football game. I wasn't that brave. I needed to find a church home that met somewhere in the middle between Pentecostal and Presbyterian.

Digging through my underwear drawer the following Sunday, I found a pair of pantyhose. Then I pulled a wool skirt from the back of my closet where the career clothes hung out, waiting to make an appearance if the stay-at-home mom gig didn't work out. The skirt fit tight, and the entire matter of church shopping felt rather constraining, but Kati's eternity was in my hands. "Wish me luck," I called over my shoulder as Chuck jiggled our daughter on his knee. She giggled and so did I. Luck had nothing to do with it.

Our church had to be out there somewhere, one that taught the honest-to-goodness truth without a set of invisible rules. On a whim, I turned north toward my hometown and let the car take me where it may. I guess muscle memory took over, because I ended up back where my faith had begun. According to the worn sign by the road, I was ten minutes late for service. I only hesitated briefly before making up my mind. It was like going back in time.

My heels clicked on the patched asphalt of the parking lot where I first squealed my teenage tires. Adult legs labored steep steps that my younger self used to take two at a time. I pulled on the door handle, relieved to find it unlocked for the prodigal who stepped over the threshold and into the vestibule. Nothing had changed except the church's name, its pastor, and the new believers who dwelled in the pews. The encounter was like having a dream where you know you're home but everything's different. You hope you'll be able to describe it after you wake.

My old congregation had vacated the pews of this building years ago, exchanging them for cushioned folding chairs and upgrading the sound system. Had the microphone that chased my testimony made the transition to the new space? I hoped so.

Laughter ringing from inside the sanctuary struck me as odd. Had I stumbled into some New Age denomination? I double-checked the masthead on the bulletin the usher had thrust at me on my late arrival, then I proceeded with relief. Slipping into the last pew of Community Bible Church, I casually set my Bible beside me as a barrier against any overzealous Christian intent on saving a stranger's soul. *Back off, sister,* the Bible would say to a potential intruder. *I've been here before. I know the drill.*

Words to a familiar praise song flashed on the screen above the worship leader at the pulpit. I closed my eyes and moved my mouth, proving I knew every verse. At the chorus repeat, I slyly peeked around to see if any parishioners from the old days had decided to stay through the church's transition. I didn't recognize anyone. I was safe.

At the song's end, the worship leader invited us all to the front. I panicked. *Not this again.* Even as I followed people stepping out into the aisles and walking toward the altar, I considered an exit strategy. Before anyone noticed, I could be in my car, heading home to lunch with my little family. Sundays were meant to be spent with family, not with people who pretended to be family until you didn't measure up. But I was too late.

"Hi! I'm Sherre. Are you new here, too?" A pretty woman that appeared to be my age turned to face me and grabbed my hands, her enthusiasm bubbling over into my guarded space.

"Mmm hmm," I responded with a thin smile, crossing my arms, and looking away.

Then my eye followed a man I didn't recognize as he stepped down into the baptismal tank. He wore a blue satin choir robe no doubt left behind by our old gospel choir. A plain wooden cross hung on the wall behind him, the same cross that shadowed me for years. That cross knew how many times I'd waded into those icy waters to proclaim my love for Jesus, each time so sure *this* baptism would be for good, a new beginning.

"Hey, how's everyone doing? What a day, huh? I bet you all would rather be out on the golf course. I know I would!" The man chuckled, and so did everyone else. I discreetly looked around. What was different here? I decided to stay and find out what it was.

"Well, welcome to Community Bible. I'm Pastor Tom. I asked you all down front today because one of our dear sisters has asked to be baptized. Linda?" He turned to the right and extended his hand. A striking brunette accepted it, bravely descending into the waist-deep water with a splash and a "Brr!" The crowd giggled again; this time, I joined in. But the laughs subsided as the pastor's face took on a serious expression.

"Linda, do you believe that Jesus Christ is the Savior of the world?" She nodded. "Is Jesus Christ your Savior, Linda?"

She nodded profusely. "Yes, oh yes." Then she plugged her nose, tears streaming down her face.

"Then, my dear sister, upon your profession of faith, I baptize you in the name of the Father, the Son, and the Holy Spirit." Linda disappeared, falling back into the water while Pastor Tom guided her immersion, employing physical strength and powerful words. "Buried with Him in baptism, raised to new life in Christ." When she emerged, a cheer erupted from the crowd, the loudest yelp coming from my new acquaintance Sherre, followed by enthusiastic applause.

The soaking-wet believer raised her arms in victory and mouthed *Thank you, Jesus.* The sermon hadn't been delivered yet, but the message was clear. Going all-in with Jesus was to be received freely and celebrated, not worked for in a spirit of dread. I wanted my children to grow up in a church like that.

As I made my way back to the pew, it felt like I was floating, and I could tell by the looks on the faces around me that I wasn't alone. Shortly, Pastor Tom returned to the stage wearing dry clothes, a Bible in hand. I don't remember the sermon preached or passage read, but I recall a part of the prayer that took hold of my heart in a way like never before and invited me to open it to Jesus again.

"Lord Jesus, we're here because we believe You are who You say You are. You came from Heaven to earth, lived a perfect life, then died for our sins because You loved us. We believe You were stone-cold dead and got up and walked out of the grave because You are the Son of God.

"We're not perfect, but we're yours, Jesus. Most of the time, we're like the walking wounded. Help us live for You. Walk among us as You've promised, changing our hearts, changing our minds. Change our lives in Your gentle, loving way."

Pastor Tom closed the prayer like a teacher leading his students to the answer they already knew by heart. "And all God's people said . . ."

Without overthinking it, I answered like everyone else around me. "Amen!"

It was true; I'd known Jesus and been known by Him all along. I'd been wounded along the way, stumbled around a bit, but I'd never been knocked off the right path. Sometimes, life has to come full circle before you realize where you belong.

* * *

"What'd you do at Nanny's today?" I asked the kids in the rearview mirror. Peanut butter, sand, and a little mischief were smeared across their faces. Why would such a meticulous woman allow her grandchildren to be released back to my care unkempt? It must be a payback of some sort.

"Nanny goes round and round," my three-year-old son announced.

"What does that mean?" I pictured Mom with her arms out, twirling like a top in the summer breeze. There was no limit to what she'd do to make her grandkids grin.

"She doesn't know how to get to the toy store," big sister clarified, "so she keeps turning right."

"Nanny goes round and round," her brother repeated with a shrug and shake of his head.

* * *

Still emotionally dizzy after circling Mom's block so many times and failing to find entry because of the church crowd, I pulled back into my own driveway as frustrated as Nanny must have been that day when she couldn't get to where she wanted to go.

Nanny goes round and round; so did I.

When it's important to get where you're going, you keep coming back.

I learned that from her.

Chapter 5

Finding A Way

After a restless night, morning broke, and I decided that today I'd see Mom, no matter what. This time, the driveway was empty. Dad opened the door. I hugged him, but not for long. It was her that I came to see. Mom sat at her usual spot at the kitchen table, brown wavy hair carefully parted, lipstick and mascara applied, a cup of coffee in her neat, manicured hands. But her eyes were downcast, ashamed. She looked as if she might crumble with one wrong word.

"Mom" was all I could think to say. I stood behind her, one hand hovering over her shoulder. When she didn't turn to me, I pressed on with a gingerly embrace, encompassing her stiff spine and the chair's carved spindles. I held the hug, not caring how much the hardness hurt. After a while, she reached up and squeezed my arm with one hand.

Our hugs were awkward like that, as if each of us was afraid the other might break the frail treaty between us. But with that one touch from her, hope began to trickle, and my thirsty soul gulped what it could. I didn't want to let go, though the cancer waiting around the corner demanded to be addressed.

Mom cleared her throat. "I'm sorry, Nikki."

Her apology made no sense. Why was she sorry for a disease she didn't cause? She had little remorse for the hurt she caused me in the past but was apologetic for what she had no control over? "I should have gone to the doctor sooner. I thought the rash would go away."

Dad was perched on his usual chair, waiting for an opening. "Your mother even visited a tanning bed! Can you believe that? She thought the sunlamps might heal her skin." Dad wore a dazed smile like he'd been practicing positivity in the mirror for hours. God bless him. He was forever looking on the bright side.

We laughed a little, me remembering Mom's furrowed brow at all my efforts to obtain the perfect shade of golden-brown skin. If there were two roads to choose from, Mom generally chose the one less traveled. Much of her glowing skin hadn't seen the sun since age fourteen, and she never drank a drop of alcohol or puffed a cigarette. She lined up her vitamins alphabetically and downed them with neat sips of distilled water. Mom could spell *homeopathic* long before natural medicine was trendy. It was astounding that this same woman disrobed, laid down in a tanning bed, and let hot lights blast her virgin white skin in a desperate attempt to make cancer go away.

I stopped laughing and sat at the table, too. She must be terrified.

"What kind of breast cancer?" I dared ask. Mom lost her mother to a slow-growing breast cancer that had given their broken relationship years to heal. Maybe the same would be true for us, something good out of something terrible.

"Inflammatory." Mom stared into her cold coffee, one thumb rubbing lipstick from the rim.

I wondered if she was thinking the same thing I was. Chuck's relative had died of that same rare cancer at thirty-nine years old.

43

"I'm sorry," she repeated, beginning to cry.

"It's not your fault." I jumped up to hug her again, this time crouching low and sideways, threading one arm behind her back and in front of the stupid chair, determined to find a way to bring her closer. She sat unmoving except for the force of silent sobs. I longed to pull her close, to squeeze her tight so she could feel the fierce love that welled up inside me, but I held back. Experience warned me not to lean too hard toward her or draw too close. But I'd always wanted to believe that our relationship could be different someday. Why not today?

I'd rehearsed a speech in the dark the night before, sensing the minutes slowly tick away. *I'm scared, Mom*, I'd planned to say, *but I'm here for you. We'll face this together, you and me. I'll be the daughter you always wanted me to be.*

But when the push of a ripe moment for vulnerable words came to shove, I was a coward. "I should get back to the kids." I traced a flower on the plastic placemat before me, looking for an exit in the maze of emotions suddenly laid out on the table.

My heart was always torn in two. I could never connect it. Here was Mom, an arms-length away, her whole life coming apart, and I wanted to bolt, run home, lock the doors, and hold my children.

Oh! My kids! I didn't know how to tell them this kind of news. To them, Nanny was ice cream sundaes, sleepovers, and giggles. She was a soft, welcoming embrace and the enthusiastic recipient of animated conversations and dandelion bouquets. Their Nanny was the doting grandma I longed for as a child, but never had.

More than once, when Kati slept over at Nanny's, she was allowed to exercise her alter ego aptly named "Bad Kati." My mom braced the floor lamp with one hand and pulled Kati close with the other, calling for my dad to grab anything not nailed down before proceeding with a soon-infamous question. "Are you Good Kati or Bad Kati tonight?"

Whatever the answer, both versions of Kati, good or bad, were welcome at Nanny's. Dumbfounded at hearing of the exchange, I was left to wonder if unconditional love sometimes skipped a generation, waiting for a more deserving soul. That puzzle was too much to figure out in a lifetime, let alone on one morning tainted by a diagnosis of cancer.

When I stood to go, Dad also stood, ever the gentleman, even when his world was falling apart. I gave him a quick hug, afraid the grief inflicting the heart I felt rapidly beating in his chest might be contagious. I loved him too much to risk absorbing his pain and coming undone.

I refused to let weakness happen. Mom and Dad had done what they could to give me a firm foundation. It was time to return the favor. I'd be strong for us all.

The following week, I sat next to Dad in a waiting room furnished with tan chairs, their squared-off wooden arms separating huddles of families and friends waiting for news from beyond the white wall of the surgery ward.

Dad and I didn't say much, only what was necessary. We settled in, taking cues from people around us, who took sips of lukewarm coffee from Styrofoam cups and held steady at the sight of surgical scrubs, waiting for their loved one's name to be called. I glanced at my watch. It would be a while.

Dad propped Mom's Bible on his knee, his trembling, freckled hand securing the book from falling to the floor. He also guarded her purse at his feet. Dad was used to balancing and carrying the items Mom needed as she vacillated between faith and fear. He operated the same way at church, following her down the aisle with her Bible and handbag, oblivious to other men's snickers. He'd bear any burden for her, but how much can one person carry?

I leafed through a stack of old *Woman's Day* magazines, scanning its ideas for making daily life better: "Clean the House in Fifteen Minutes," "Pack a Healthy Lunch," "Tone Your Arms Using Canned Goods for Weights." Up until the last crinkled issue in the stack, I held out hope the slick pages would yield wisdom for what I faced in the unforeseeable future.

What had I thought I'd discover inside the magazine? "Ten Steps to Improve Your Faith Walk (Even If You Aren't Sure You Have One)"? "Five Reasons Your Mom Loves You More Than You Think"? "Three Short Prayers for Desperate Times"? The wrinkled, glossy pages offered nothing to help me. Setting down the last magazine, I craned my neck for a vending machine. What I needed was a Diet Coke.

"Need anything?" I asked.

Dad looked up at me, his usually bright turquoise eyes dulled from pain. Mom's agony was his own. He opened his mouth to speak, then changed his mind. What he needed was a miracle.

"Mr. Bliss?" A woman wearing a white coat and holding a clipboard invited Dad through an open doorway. My eternally young father, usually capable of springing to his toes on a moment's notice, struggled to stand. I jumped to my feet too quickly, grabbed for the arm of a chair, and found Dad's arm instead. After we steadied each other, I let him walk ahead as I followed in a disconnected trance, counting each step. One, two, three, four. Maybe I'd never arrive and could walk all the way home, forgetting cancer ever happened to our family.

That wish collapsed at sight of the doctor who sat waiting behind a desk. I smiled a nervous smile she didn't return. She looked as dark as the hair peeking out of her surgical cap. *Zero bedside manner.* I decided they must consider expanding the medical field to include handling human emotion. I glared back at her until I remembered Mom's life was in this woman's hands.

The doctor wasted no time with small talk, directing her attention to Dad. "Your wife's in recovery now. The surgery was more extensive than we anticipated. We removed her breast and several lymph nodes that appeared cancerous. The lab is testing them now." She continued talking, but I couldn't take in any more information. The cancer had gone farther into Mom's body than anyone thought.

This was an uncommon phenomenon. Nothing ever got past Mom. When it came to faith, she could batten down the hatches against evil better than anyone.

Our first family home sat on a busy street close to town, so our front door was a frequent target of Jehovah's Witnesses hoping to include us in their end-time tally. As the Vietnam War raged on, they became more fervent in their knocking but soon found out that Mom was equally passionate about God's Word and the Second Coming of Christ. To protect my little brother and me from their false doctrine, she stepped out onto the porch, gently pulled the door closed behind her, and went to work disputing their arguments. She remained standing as the unannounced visitors and demons fled.

Mom's friends admired her tenacity, labeling their righteous friend "bold as a lion"[6] But as her daughter, I observed her more human side. All it took was one small shadow scurrying across the kitchen carpet, and she was up on a chair screaming like a banshee. Dad set trap after trap, but keeping the mouse population down in a drafty house built in 1895 was next to impossible.

So, Mom adopted a faith strategy. She would ban the mice by disbelief in their presence. No one was to talk about a mouse, spot a mouse, or say that leaving a crumb out on the kitchen counter might draw mice that didn't exist. The strategy kept Mom's peace until one time after she left the dishes soaking in the sink overnight. Bleary-eyed the next morning, she grabbed the "sponge" and took

---

[6] Proverbs 28:1 (NIV).

hold of a reality she'd managed to avoid.

Foundations like Mom's mouse strategy can develop cracks through which some unwanted visitors manage to get in. You can't deny what you don't want to exist. Somehow, you have to face a reality no matter how much it scares you.

While I believed faith wasn't true faith if it didn't hold up to questions, Dad was asking the doctor questions that weren't pertinent to the aggressive plan needed to fight for Mom's life. "When can she go home? What can she eat? Is it OK to go to church?" I needed to cut to the chase. What were we really dealing with here? Brought into the open, I could fight it. The unseen scared me, the unknown little scratching feet inside the walls.

"So, Doctor, exactly how big was the tumor you removed? What stage is the cancer? How long until she beats this?" The questions fired off my lips.

The doctor turned to face me directly, her brow furrowed with frustration. Perhaps my parents hadn't told me something I should have known. She looked irritated by my inquisition, but I no longer cared. I stared back at her, holding her brown eyes without a blink. *Bring it.*

"Her breast," the doctor answered.

"Yes, I know," I smiled pleasantly to hide my impatience. "She has cancer of the breast, but how big was the *tumor* in her breast?" Clearly, the doctor and I were having trouble communicating.

"Her entire breast. Her entire breast was a tumor."

The fear suspended over my heart took aim and started swinging. How much hope had been extinguished in this very room? Where'd the doctor bury all the victims? No one could leave here after hearing this kind of news.

"Inflammatory cancer is very aggressive. By the time the rash appears, it's too late to contain. I'm sorry."

I stood to leave, walking wounded. But fear wanted to make

sure this was a thorough execution. "Because of the hard lymph nodes discovered," the doctor added, "I'm labeling this as Stage 4." Mom's cancer was lethal.

Feeling my way along a row of chairs to my seat in the waiting area, I noticed every stranger's head bowed in the room. Did they overhear the news? Were they already praying for Mom? A sinking realization came. Witnessing another human's suffering, they feared they might be next.

Nearby, a woman moaned softly, then louder and louder until her moan turned into a wail. Unable to see where she sat, I groped for an unoccupied chair and collapsed into it clumsily. From my sitting position, I caught sight of the young woman out of the corner of my eye. She rocked back and forth, holding her head, making a complete spectacle of her sorrow. I watched helplessly, nothing left in me to give anyone else.

An old hymn began to play in my memory, one Mommy used to sing to soothe my nightmares. It flowed from my lips in whispered squeaks, the melody I could manage off-key.

> "Peace! peace! wonderful peace,
> Coming down from the Father above;
> Sweep over my spirit forever, I pray,
> In fathomless billows of love."[7]

Fathomless billows was a phrase from a long-ago time, words with meaning I'd never considered. Now I understood them. Fathomless billows were what I couldn't escape, waves of sorrow slamming me up against hard news I'd prayed wouldn't come. I began to cry, drowning in sorrow like the girl next to me. *Help us, Lord Jesus,* I pled, because neither one of us could help the other.

Dad's voice parted the deep waters, thin but steady, traveling

---

[7] "Wonderful Peace" by W. D. Cornell, Melodies of Praise Hymnal (1957).

a stream of hope from the open Bible in his hand. "My thoughts are not your thoughts. Neither are your ways, My ways, declares the Lord." I turned toward the sound of his voice, allowing God's Word to wash over me.

The wailing receded, and the love of God rose up and flooded my heart, alternate fathomless billows reminding me of His greatness and making me feel small. I experienced the soothing in the melody I'd been singing. *Peace, peace, wonderful peace.*

The distraught woman in me that had appeared out of nowhere stepped aside, and a newer, calmer version of who I was becoming took her place. A verse flashed through my mind. *Faith comes by hearing, and hearing by the word of God.*[8]

OK, Lord. I'm ready to listen.

Dad's voice grew stronger as he continued to annunciate the words of Isaiah 55. "For as far as the heavens are above the earth, so are my ways above your ways and my thoughts above your thoughts."[9]

Contrary to what I grew up believing, God's ways didn't avoid the valley of the shadow of death. God's ways would take me straight through it along with Mom. You can let the good in even if you can't keep the bad out.

I learned that from her.

---

[8] Romans 10:17 (NKJV).
[9] Isaiah 55:8–9 (NIV).

Chapter 6

Flesh and Blood

Mom began chemotherapy treatments to eradicate cancer, and I set out to become a better version of myself.

"Applesauce carrots, corn, peaches, peas, pineapple." I stood back to survey my work in the pantry. Each can was perfectly aligned. Excellent.

Like Mom, I loved alphabetizing and categorizing my world. But when I turned to tackle the dirty dishes, two leftover cans remained on the counter, posing a dilemma. Where would I put fruit cocktail and mixed vegetables? They didn't fit the pattern.

To me, clear thinking demanded order; order required separation; separation necessitated constant vigilance. In a fast-moving household of four people, the order I strived for got all mixed up. With everyone usually moving in different directions, it felt like I should be in two places at the same time. That was impossible, so chaos was inevitable unless I found a workaround.

The solution was two sets of everything—indoor and outdoor dishes, bath and beach towels, dance and school bags, Mom's "Spirit-filled" beliefs and my traditional ones, friends who liked to party distinct from friends who wanted to talk about Jesus. With my heart split in two in many situations and relationships, I offered whichever half circumstances deemed appropriate. Holy Nikki attended church, read her Bible, squeezed hands in prayer circles, and truly loved the Lord. Holy Nikki held her breath until her family pulled out of the church parking lot. Then Human Nikki began to take over. Some Sundays, keeping up the holy facade proved more challenging because of the other people in the car.

"Aerosmith? Really, Chuck? Can you turn that crap down?"

"Dad! Mom said *crap!*" I'd glare at Chuck, then adjust the visor's mirror so I could stare down my giggling kids as we rolled past the pastor's car.

Inevitably, Chuck would roll down the window to chat, and Holy Nikki would return the pastor's smile. "Great sermon, Pastor Tom. Really, really good!" Holy Nikki's sentences ended at a higher pitch as if pointing to Heaven. Holy Nikki tried harder to stick around longer each week but started to wonder. Was it a sin to be human? Both Holy Nikki and Human Nikki seemed to think so.

Driving to the store one day, I flipped through radio stations and landed on a preacher addressing his audience in an accusatory tone. "Do you put God in a box and only take Him out on Sunday?" Though I immediately turned the dial, the question remained. How does one do it any other way? My church friends didn't seem to have a conflict. They were 100 percent in with Jesus every day of the week.

My cell phone rang, interrupting my thoughts. "Hey, want to come to BSF?" My friend Penny, one of those people in with Jesus 100 percent, offered her annual invitation for me to become a better Christian. *Weird timing.*

"BSF stands for Bible Study Fellowship," Penny explained. To me, the meetings sounded misery-inducing.

Human Nikki had way too much to do; frankly, she was more comfortable with a life that she could arrange herself. But Holy

Nikki knew she had to get life in a higher order so God would accept her prayers to heal her mom.

"Sure?" I wasn't confident, but sometimes you have no choice. I could always quit if the fellowship got too churchy. The following Tuesday, I gathered supplies. Bible? Notebook? Highlighter? Holy Nikki? Check, check, check, check. As Lynn's daughter, I had a good idea of what items to bring to a Bible study. What eluded me were the answers.

Mom's Bible traveled from the nightstand to the kitchen table every morning so she could sit and have coffee with God. She'd copy verses onto lined index cards that later lay on the window sill above the kitchen sink, so she could think about them as she wiped the daily grime off the dinner dishes. Mom was ready if anyone had a question about Jesus and His love for them at any point of the day.

It was maddening. Just once, I wanted Mom to give me her honest opinion about anything. Just once, I wanted to see a crack in her holy armor and have a human conversation without God speaking for her. The God conversations were one-sided. One day, I hoped to hear from an actual human on the other line.

What would Jesus do? We're told to ask ourselves that, but being holy must have been easier for Jesus. After all, He was God's Son; I was Lynn's daughter.

* * *

In 1969, the chairs used for our Sunday School were flesh-colored but cold as steel. It took great effort not to squirm as the teacher told the Bible story. Since the story was always somehow about the Son of God, wiggles were out of the question.

Sister Baker moved colorful cut-out Bible characters across a flannel-covered board to hold our attention. Even so, imagining Jesus as an actual live human was hard. His paper image looked flat as the board it was stuck to and wore the same one-dimensional expression whether suffering on the cross or standing triumphant by the tomb. Flat Jesus never strayed far and always spoke from Scripture. Even His toes were on point.

Being holy like Jesus felt impossible. More worrisome, nothing about Jesus seemed human like me.

* * *

I arrived at BSF five minutes late, overwhelmed by the steep steps I had to climb to reach the door. Why did God make it so hard to get to Him? Breathless from the climb, I accepted a name tag and hurried to my assigned room.

Connie was the leader of our little group. Like Pastor Tom, she was different in the best kind of way. She didn't mention my tardiness but greeted me with an easy smile. "OK, folks, let's crack open that Bible to the book of Romans and see what God has to say." Her brows raised over kind, mischievous eyes that indicated studying the Bible might be fun.

I wasn't so sure about that. Sweat broke out on my forehead.

A studious woman volunteered to read the first assigned verse. "I am not ashamed of the gospel."[10] My heart skipped a beat. I *was* ashamed of the gospel, because I was ashamed of the human parts of me, the parts I couldn't control all the time. I rarely told people outside of church that I was a Christian, because there were times I didn't act like one. I didn't want anyone to get the wrong idea about Jesus because of me. I didn't want to ruin His reputation.

"The righteous will live by faith,"[11] another woman reported, reading where the first one left off. I listened with the familiar shame that came with knowing better but not doing better. I had to figure out how to try harder to live by faith, even if I had to wrestle Human Nikki to the ground and smother her with a pillow.

I couldn't breathe as the following verses rattled off a checklist

---

[10] Romans 1:16 (NIV).
[11] Romans 1:17 (NIV).

of sins, some unthinkable to me, others hitting a little too close to home: envy, murder, strife, deceit, malice, gossips, slanderers, God-haters, insolent, arrogant and boastful, disobedient to their parents.[12] Mom's face inevitably appeared.

"Nikki, are you comfortable reading verse 32 of this chapter?" Connie asked.

"Of course." After all, I'd earned at least a million gold stars from reading Bible verses over the years. "Although they know God's righteous decree that those who do such things deserve death, they not only continue to do these very things but also approve of those who practice them."[13] Smiling awkwardly, I hoped I didn't have to provide commentary. I wasn't ignorant of what God required, only incapable of pulling it off.

After the discussion concluded, Connie passed out the following week's lesson. I was mortified as I glanced at the homework in my hand. There were only questions, no answers. What if I didn't know a right response?

Later, I laid the homework aside and placed my daily check-in call to Mom. "How was your first BSF class?" she asked. I imagined she'd been waiting all day to find out.

"Fine, I guess. Pretty good." The little lie seemed prudent. I didn't want to share or discuss my doubts with Mom, our family's resident Bible scholar. My uncertainty would cause her to believe I wasn't a bona fide, tried-and-true believer, so I switched to a more comfortable subject—for me. "How was chemo?"

Mom rose to answer without skipping a beat. "Good. Going well. I'm healed in Jesus's name." Her reply was automatic, because she believed a confession of holy faith was more powerful than any fate the human world tried to hand her. I struggled to believe like she did; my prayers were never considered spiritual enough.

---

[12] Romans 1:29–30 (NIV).
[13] Romans 1:32 (NIV).

"Our whole church is praying for you, Mom." That was a big deal, right? It involved the whole church, not just a few people gathered in a corner at the altar. That past Sunday, I'd faced my fear of raising my hand in church and asked for prayer in front of the entire congregation.

"That's nice," she said flatly, as if I'd told her someone would be sending her a bill for a routine service call regarding an appliance.

My upbringing told me that prayers were only powerful if they were uttered through the Holy Ghost. The limitation didn't stop me from praying, but it kept me from believing God heard me.

During the period when Mom was believing so hard for a miracle, I determined it was better to avoid looking her in the eye. Her Holy Spirit vision could see through me, and I feared what she saw would disappoint her. So, I found ways to show I cared without seeing her.

Cleanliness is next to godliness. While that saying was not a Bible verse, Mom obeyed it as if it were. A scrub brush was the way to her heart. I chose to appeal to her fastidiousness with a surprise house cleaning.

"Hello? Mom? Dad?" I peeked my head into Mom's laundry room and waited. The emptiness that echoed through the house confirmed I had arrived in time. They were gone to chemo. I could clean the house before they returned.

I swung the heavy bucket of cleaning supplies on the counter and looked around. They must have left in a hurry. If Mom had known I was coming, she would've never left the house so untidy. Even if she had to pull herself out of bed to vomit, she'd return to make her bed—corners of the sheet folded sharply, blanket smoothed, pillows fluffed.

I remembered the days I followed Mom around the house with my toy broom and dust-pan. I proudly mimicked her every move. That's how little girls learn. I wasn't sure how Mom learned to keep such a meticulous house. She had no one to follow.

* * *

I followed the click of Mommy's heels down the outside stairwell, past a grimy window where a Siamese cat staring at me from in the flat arched its back, its fangs bared in a silent hiss warning us not to enter. Mommy knocked on the door and waited. She knocked again, looking back at Daddy. Then she shielded her squint and pressed her face against the window, trying to see inside.

"I think she's in there," she muttered to herself, cracking the door open as if afraid of what she might find. "Mother? Are you in here? It's Lynn." Mommy entered and we followed.

A lean silhouette sat rigid at the kitchen table, staring into space. One might've thought she was a mannequin if it weren't for the constant tapping of her foot. She held a lit cigarette a few inches from thin red lips parted to let the smoke escape. From her clothing—a long pencil skirt, snagged hose, scuffed pumps, and a pillbox hat perched on frizzy hair—it appeared she'd been on her way out the door and then decided against it.

"Mother, have you eaten today?" Mommy asked, glancing around at the disaster that unveiled itself begrudgingly in the dusky smoke. A few cats prowled the kitchen counter, weaving in and out of a maze of half-empty lipstick-stained coffee cups and cans of cat food with jagged lids propped open. The cats held their tails high, as if proud of the dirty dishes in the sink and of the old magazines and cigarette cartons littering the table.

The Siamese cat I'd seen hissing from the window earlier jumped to the floor and pressed against my legs, asking to be petted. "Nikki, don't touch the kitty. Don't touch anything. Warren, can you please watch her?"

"I had coffee," Grandma mumbled, interrupting the ruckus, peering at her daughter through smudged cat-eye glasses.

"Now, Mother, you need to eat." Mommy opened the

refrigerator and blanched, her manicured fingers discreetly covering her nose at the sour assault. She quickly closed the door and turned to face us with an odd smile.

"Let's see if we can get this place cleaned up before we go find some breakfast."

I wasn't hungry. I wanted to get in the car and drive back home.

* * *

After taking in the unusual sights of a sink filled with dirty dishes and coffee cups sitting on the kitchen table, I headed to Mom's room to assess her health by the state of the bed. It was made. I sighed with relief.

Medicine bottles and bandages cluttered the nightstand next to her Bible. I picked up a bottle and read the instructions. *Take two pills as needed.* Unwilling to think of how many she must need, I set the bottle back on the nightstand and was surprised by the layer of dust.

While I moved the bottles and Bible onto the bed so I could wipe the nightstand, a piece of paper fell out of the Bible and fluttered to the floor. It bore Mom's unmistakable penmanship, neat blue loops of ink that flowed with her thoughts. Because it was tucked in her Bible, I knew it was personal, her note to the Lord. I shouldn't have read it, but I was hungry to know what she was thinking, not what she thought I should hear. If it was a prayer list, I feared seeing my name at the top but hoped I'd made the cut.

After glancing around the corner to ensure no one was coming, I snatched the paper up like a hundred-dollar bill and scanned the list.

> Husband
> Children
> Grandchildren to 1,000 generations

A thousand generations? I swallowed hard, imagining Kati and

Chapin with children of their own. Leave it to Mom to think so far ahead.

As I tucked the list back in the Bible, the weighty meaning beneath that last line hit me hard. Raised in the church, I knew what the phrase "1,000 generations" meant. Mom was basing her prayers on a promise of God that followed the Second Commandment. Disobedience would result in a generational curse, "punishing the children for the sin of the fathers to the third and fourth generation,"[14] but loving God above all else would result in a stream of love that would never end, "but showing love to a thousand generations of those who love me and keep my commandments."[15] I set the alarm clock back on the nightstand, the second hand seeming to gain speed as it swept past each number. I needed to get my act together in more ways than one.

Bucket swinging from my forearm like a purse, I moved through the tiny house at top speed, the way she had taught me. Start high, finish low. Lift, wipe, reach into the corner; don't stop short. Empty the trash can and wipe it down. Pull the doors shut; push the drawers closed. It had been almost twenty years since I'd lived with her, but I knew the home's orderly rhythm and what it took to achieve her standard.

A glance at my watch urged me to move faster, one more room to go. I charged into the bathroom, sprayed the mirror, wiped the counter, and swapped out the hand towel. Seeing a shiny object peeking out from the makeup drawer stopped me in my tracks. I caressed the gold lipstick tube, thinking it strange that she hadn't taken it. Mom never went anywhere without a tube in her bag. Next to Jesus, the perfect shade of red lipstick was her highest pursuit.

According to family folklore, her lipstick had been a siren song

---

[14] Exodus 20:5 (NIV).
[15] Exodus 20:6 (NIV).

to me since I was little. During a summer road trip when I was three, Mommy's purse sat beside me in the back seat. Throughout the drive, I was quiet as a mouse and good as gold. My parents couldn't believe their fine fortune in having such a perfect child, until they glanced over their shoulders and saw the truth. God had delivered a flawed human to their doorstep.

Mommy's neatly lined crimson lips turned down at the sight of my first failed attempt at wearing lipstick. She grabbed a tissue and wiped the makeup off my lips, cheeks, and chin. I wanted to be like her, but I couldn't color inside the lines.

Some things never change. I rolled up the tube to reveal a muted burgundy, ran a pinky over the waxy stick, then swept the finger across my bottom lip. *Hmm, not bad.*

Snapping back to reality, I opened the shower curtain. As expected, a white washcloth was squeezed of excess moisture and neatly folded over the spout. That was her rule, so ingrained in me that I demanded it in my own bathroom, but the family's resistance was infuriating. At least one wet washcloth discarded in a careless heap greeted me every morning. *"Why?* Why can't you do it right?" I'd force my anger through grinding teeth and squeeze every drop down the drain, then give the cloth a few quick shakes before folding it corner to corner and draping it across the spout. By now, didn't they know better than to leave a mess for someone else to clean? In fact, a person should go one step farther and remove all evidence that you needed cleansing in the first place.

I learned that from her.

I began to pull the curtain closed when I noticed something amiss. The drain was black, not silver. Keeping my eyes on the darkness, I reached back, groping to find the toilet paper, grateful to have seen the affront before her.

Even layered with a mountain of wadded tissue, the clump of walnut-brown hair refused to be covered. I grabbed the wad and squeezed, the dampness of the repulsive prize soaking through the tissue and molding it to my fist, making me gag. The find had to be carried away, as far away as possible. Like a solemn pallbearer, I held the wad at arm's length and dropped it in the trash with a thud. Pulling the bag out, I knotted it—once, twice, three times. Then I carried the bag into the garage, pushed it deep down to the bottom of the metal garbage can so she couldn't find it, and pressed the lid closed, using all my weight as a seal.

Her secret was safe with me, although it haunted me no matter how far I shoved it into my subconscious. I ran hot water into the kitchen sink until steam rose, then I plunged my soapy hands under the flow. The sight of Mom's mortality made me feel dirty and wrung my soul bone dry.

Before walking out the door, I scribbled a note. "I was here. Cleaned the house. Hope you don't mind. I love you. Me."

I sped off in one direction as they pulled into the driveway from another, happy to have pulled off my surprise. But my heart told me it couldn't keep living this way. One day, Mom and I would have to admit that we were only human.

The reckoning was inevitable.

Between me and Mom. Between me and Jesus. Between me and me.

A few weeks later, it began.

Chapter 7

A Different View

"What are you watching? Turn it off!" I stepped into the living room and the kids scattered, leaving the TV blaring with the ear-piercing screams of a woman running through the woods, an ax-wielding monster hot on her heels. "You're not supposed to watch horror movies!" I called up the stairs to the guilty parties now hiding. "They're from the devil!" I added for effect.

It was true. Evil was real and showed up when you least expected it. To prevent the inevitable was a mother's job, but I was terrified I couldn't. Halloween was right around the corner, and I received a lot of pushback for my refusal to make it into a holiday. "Mom, why can't we hang up ghosts and witches like the neighbors?"

"Because I said so." I told Chuck, "I have no idea why I live in such fear, I had a perfect childhood."

"No, you didn't," he challenged, one to talk. What I knew about his childhood trauma made my blood run cold. Because of his past, he saw glimpses into mine that I refused to see.

Every family has its demons. Some entertain them, foolishly believing their family won't get burned. Others pretend evil doesn't exist, unable to fathom that a good God could let bad things happen. Still others choose to go head-to-head with their demons, determined to outwit and outpower them in a fight for their lives. The more timid bunch I belong to knows spiritual forces are plotting to destroy us, so we do our best not to attract evil's attention. Above all else, I desired to keep my little family out of the firing line.

* * *

Mom knew there was a devil. She'd looked him in the eye and saw he wanted to steal her hope and her faith, but she was determined not to let him have them. That's why she let me ride shotgun on a "demon fighting" mission one summer day rather than leave me home unprotected. I waited in the back seat while she and her prayer partner visited the poor soul needing deliverance. "We won't be long, honey," she said, and she was right.

They returned quickly, pale-faced and flustered. I leaned forward to hear their panicked whispers. "I plead the blood of Jesus on this car! I take authority over the powers of darkness in Jesus's name!" The story came out while we raced back to the church for reinforcements. A demon had ripped the Bible in two before their very eyes. If God couldn't stop a demon from tearing apart His Word, would I be next?

Mom locked the car doors, but I wasn't sure that would keep the devil out. My only ride with the "Ghost Buster" squad taught me it would take more than that.

After that fateful day, Mom decided I'd be safer at home, but demons were everywhere. I was drawn to scary movies, eyes glued to the TV screen while my little heart beat wildly. The villain impacting me most was a severed hand that crept down a bedroom hallway toward innocent sleeping children.

The film spawned a recurring nightmare in which a hand chased me out into the yard, backed me into a corner, and began to choke me. I opened my mouth to call for help, but no sound came out. No one could hear me. No one was coming to save me.

I woke Mom with my screams, and she always came running, even when she was dealing with a nightmare of her own.

* * *

Grandma's visit was uneventful until all hell broke loose.

"You called me a BITCH!" Grandma bellowed. She ran up the stairs wildly, appearing in my room.

"Now, Mother, calm down. That's not true." Mommy appeared on the scene, crouching as she moved toward me, warily watching, slowly stepping backward until she stood between me and Grandma.

"I heard you talking on the phone!" Grandma continued her accusations. "You called me a BITCH! I heard you!"

I had heard Mommy talking on the phone earlier, too, but it was days before Grandma arrived. Mom hadn't called Grandma names, but had judged her condition all the same. "Please pray for us. My mother's coming for a visit, and I think she's demon-possessed."

Hearing that, I'd hugged my doll tightly and run to my room to find my Bible. The latter was what Mommy did when the devil was bothering her. Grabbing a red crayon, I opened the Good Book and pressed the wax over the words, verse after verse, with a trembling hand. My action hid the words instead of highlighting them.

With fear breathing down my neck at Grandma's sudden frantic appearance, I needed that Bible now, but it sat on the dresser across the room, farther than I dared to go.

Thankfully, Mommy knew how to defend me. Eyes wide open, she began to pray. "Jesus! I plead the blood of Jesus!" After calling Jesus, her lips continued to move in a soundless plea as she stood her ground. Below my window, cars whizzed past, unaware of the people inside needing rescue. Were Jesus and Mommy strong enough to save me? I had my doubts as Grandma leaned forward ready to pounce.

The static in the air subsided as quickly as the argument began. Grandma's brow and shoulders unfurrowed. "But," she sputtered in a childish voice, "I thought you said—"

"No, Mother." Mommy shook her head. "I would never say that. I can't do this anymore."

Not long after, Mommy helped Grandma pack her suitcase and set it by the front door.

* * *

I pressed the Off button on the TV remote, and the horrific scene my kids had been watching disappeared. That's how to deal with what scares you: shut it down and leave it in the past. Without considering other options, I applied this theory to most areas of life.

The following week, I walked into BSF intending to turn in my name tag. I could no longer take the pressure of pretending I was like all the other Christians there, and I was petrified of being discovered. During the small group discussion, I fought the urge to blurt out sarcasm. *Good for you, Brenda! I'm so happy your sins are forgiven, you're perfect, and your mother loves you. Congrats!*

"What happens if you keep falling short?" the lady next to Brenda asked our leader. "Does it mean you aren't saved?"

Connie's frank answer to the intriguing question surprised me. " 'There is no one righteous, not even one.'[16] That's what the Bible says. We're gonna struggle, even after we're saved. Salvation's based on Christ's perfection, not ours. Jesus said no one, not even we ourselves, can snatch us from His hand."

---

[16] Romans 3:10 (NIV).

That was a new piece of information. Salvation didn't depend on me? Why would God do that? How could He love me that much? I'd lay my life down to save my children, but would I lay my children's lives down for someone like me? Not a chance.

What kind of God would sacrifice His only Son for a flub-up like me?

A God I need and want to know.

Where'd He been all my life?

Right here, all along, waiting for this very moment.

Immediately, I understood why people shouted "Hallelujah!" and "Glory to God!" They weren't just acting holy. Praise was an appropriate response to receiving the grace of God.

From that day forward, all the demons in Hell couldn't rip the Bible out of my hands. Evil was rampant wherever I looked, but I was more determined than ever to keep learning about Jesus. I couldn't turn off the Good News if I wanted to. It felt like I was hearing it for the very first time, and it brought such peace.

Then fear came roaring back into my life and set the whole world on fire. I was enthusiastically teaching two-year-olds about Jesus in a BSF children's class on a September morning, when a plane hit the Twin Towers in New York. I was singing "Jesus Loves Me" when a second plane hit its mark.

Later that day, I decided to call the one person who knew how to pray demons away. So as not to alarm anyone, I pretended to be concerned about the growing stack of ironing that awaited me in the basement, casually descending the stairs until I rounded the corner.

"Mom, I'm scared," I whispered, our TV broadcasting minute-by-minute news of 9/11 in the background. I kept the volume turned down even though the kids had retreated to their bedrooms two stories up, far from the noise. But who was I kidding? Everyone on earth was in earshot of the new reality. The world as we knew it had blown up.

I gasped, unable to take my eyes off the screen. "Another plane hit the Pentagon." That news hit close to home. Before I came along, Mom had typed army retirement forms in that ultrasecure government building. A part of her past went up in flames.

Her calm voice smoothed my anxiety-wrinkled mind as my iron glided over the dress shirt on the board in front of me. "It's going to be OK, Nikki. You're all going to be OK. God is in control."

My hand kept moving the iron, stopping momentarily to press down on a stubborn wrinkle. Her words would've struck me as funny in a different place and time. Mom, the same woman who called 911 when a drop of nail polish remover splashed into her granddaughter's eye, was now a soldier at the ready, unaffected by end-time prophecies coming true before her eyes.

I couldn't dispute her, not then, not ever. But my heart questioned her confidence. *Is God really controlling this situation? Because it's not looking so good.*

The blurred face of a turban-wearing stranger filled the screen, closed captions interpreting his threats against the United States, home of the free and land of not-so-brave me, hiding out in my basement.

"Remember, Nikki," Mom continued. "No weapon formed against you shall prosper."[17] That familiar verse felt a little flimsy as my eyes stared at the assault rifles pointed in every direction on the screen. Up to this point, I'd only shot a BB gun.

Steam spit from shiny holes when I stood the iron up and set it aside. My labor was pointless. Did anyone need clothes pressed and starched while living in a bunker? "OK, Mom. You're right— God's in control. I'm going up to check on the kids. I love you."

I climbed the stairs into a living room still displaying evidence

---

[17] Isaiah 54:17 (NKJV).

of a scene a few hours before, when Chuck had delivered our high school freshman and our fourth grader safely back from school and into my arms. "It's going to be OK," I'd told them, hoping it wasn't a lie. The truth was that anything could happen at any time.

Footsteps pounded down the hallway above me and then the steep stairs. I braced for another disaster. Terror was revealing itself in waves. Kati crashed into me before I could make my way to her. What now? My eyes took in her tear-streaked cheeks and spiky dark lashes.

"What's wrong, honey?" I put a hand on her shoulder and attempted to lift her chin so I could see what needed fixing, but she shook me off and fell distraught onto the couch. I leaned closer to decipher her mumbling into the throw pillow.

"Coach Lisa's mad. She said I'm off the dance team if I don't come to practice tonight."

"What? That is *the* most RIDICULOUS thing I've ever heard! The president of the United States is scrambling nuclear codes in Air Force One as we speak!" My pointer finger jabbed the air above my head, emphasizing the proximity of the leader of the free world. "Don't you think dance practice can wait?"

She sat straight, stunned, looking at me like I'd driven another plane into a tower. "You don't understand!" She ran back upstairs to call someone who would.

From the moment she could wriggle out of my arms, Kati had always wanted someone other than me. Right now, she saw me as an enemy. The thought that we'd grow apart like Mom and I had was more alarming than the increasing possibility of a million foreign boots marching toward the front door.

"Honey, I'm sorry," I said a few minutes later, sheepishly stepping over the threshold to her room. I resisted the urge to add disclaimers. *I'm sorry, but you shouldn't let other people make you feel guilty. I'm sorry, but you shouldn't be so worried about what people think about you*. The excuses were endless, but shame would land squarely on her shoulders if I pushed the blame off mine. That wasn't the kind of mother I wanted to be.

I was supposed to be the adult, and adults see through the eyes of experience. She saw the immediate trauma of being let go from a team; I saw that priorities change when facing life and death. Life and love were worth some temporary pain. But she had yet to learn that. Her inexperience wasn't her fault.

Arms crossed, I waited for absolution from the princess ruling my heart, sprawled on her bed, thumbing through a *Teen Beat* magazine. I was at her mercy whether I wanted to admit it or not. More than anything, I wanted us to be on the same side, especially now that opposition was mounting. While she considered if I was worthy of one more chance, I looked out her window at the breathtaking scenery, a view I'd chosen to sacrifice unbeknownst to her. As far as she knew, this room and its view was meant for her alone.

* * *

"What d'ya think, Nik?" Chuck asked. "Should this be the master?"

There were three equally small bedrooms to choose from, two upstairs and one down at the back of the house. This room unveiled the apex of lake living. I leaned on the windowsill and stared out over the idyllic scene, picturing myself waking up to that every day—a pure taste of Heaven.

The lake was calm except for ripples made by a momma swan, confidently guiding babies along a shoreline where snapping turtles lay waiting among the reeds. Those youngsters had no idea of the danger they might face or that their fearless leader would hiss, honk, and snip at any threat that came their way. I'd heard that swans opposed vicious dogs to save their brood.

"Maybe the oldest kid should get dibs?"

I couldn't forget Kati's reaction to our big family announcement that we were moving again and going to live on a lake. Chapin cheered; Kati ran to her room and slammed the door. Her friends, her whole life, lived right next door. We'd intended to upgrade her life, not strip it away.

Maybe one day, in this room, she'd wake up, take in the view, and realize that the choices I made were because I loved her.

* * *

"Kati? Do you forgive me?" She nodded, turning a glossy page with a dramatic sigh. It was enough for me. "Thank you."

I turned to walk away, but there was more to say. "It's gonna be OK." *Me, you, your brother and dad, the dance team, your life, Nanny's life—all of it's gonna be OK somehow.*

Certainty of that after an enemy had terrorized thousands of people, robbing them of their last breath, sounded a little foolish. The definition of being OK had to extend beyond the scene right before us. Only God Himself had the perfect view.

"God's in control, y'know." Had it come to this? Sounding like my mother? Kati's head dipped slightly, which I took as her agreement. If I kept repeating the truth to her, perhaps I'd believe it, too.

A few days later, life picked up where it left off that 9/11 morning. "Have a good day, honey. See ya at the football game." Kati grabbed her bulging backpack, slammed the van door, and glanced over her shoulder at me before disappearing into the building. My final grade as a mother remained a mystery.

"You're a great Mom," Chuck assured me every day. "Look at all you do!" But doing and being weren't the same. I needed Kati to trust me enough to let me pull her close and keep her safe.

Later that afternoon, I climbed the aluminum steps of the school's football bleachers and joined other moms at our favorite spot, one row down from the top at center field, where we could watch the dance team and the game. Mom wasn't feeling good, so she'd decided to sit this one out. Had she arrived after me, she would've insisted I stay put and not move down to a lower riser. "I'm fine here," she'd say. "You sit with your friends."

Next week, I wouldn't give her the chance to dismiss me. I'd arrive early and save seats for us on the bottom row. Mom wouldn't miss that game; her granddaughter was performing at halftime. Kati hadn't been kicked off the dance team after all.

Behind the bleachers, Kati and her giggling group waited in the concession line. I observed from my perch, hoping she didn't catch me staring. Unlike me, she was happiest in the middle of the action. I admired that in her.

Despite the normalcy surrounding us, the atmosphere was fraught with news of war. Out of habit, I glanced at the scoreboard clock. The game should've started twenty minutes ago. *Did something else happen?* Bad news was unfolding at breakneck speed these days. Sadly, one had to assume the worst.

A commotion broke out in the direction of the school building. Heads turned toward the noise. Parents jumped up, ready to spring into action, scanning the horizon for a safe place to herd their young. I located Kati in the crowd, looking afraid and much too far away to reach at a moment's notice. What had we argued about that morning? How had we left each other?

Our habit was to say "I love you." *Yes, I'm sure that's the last thing I said.* If this was the end, a simple "I love you" would have to be sufficient. Three words would have to sum it up. *See you on the Other Side, honey. If I'm forced to leave you, I want you to know that sitting in the front row of your life was the best seat in the house.* I had no choice but to trust that God was in control and accept the worst possible outcome, the one I feared most of all.

Then, a football player rounded the corner carrying an

American flag hoisted high on a pole. His teammates joined him and charged toward the playing field in a red, white, and blue roar. Alongside the player bearing the Stars and Stripes, another player waved the Christian flag, displaying the cross of Christ, our sure victory throughout the ages.

The team whooped and hollered as they ran. Their courage was contagious. All of us gathered around the field clapped, stomped, and yelled at the top of our lungs, outshouting our fears, if only for a moment in time.

No one knew who'd win the game or the war; history had yet to record our futures. Yet the cross reminded us that King Jesus had already won the ultimate war and ascended to the highest throne. I had to trust that the King of kings and Lord of lords controlled every square inch of the universe from His high and holy vantage point.

I learned that from her.

Chapter 8

Home For Christmas

*N*ational Lampoon's Christmas Vacation provided a nice escape from the reality I faced from Thanksgiving Day through December. The movie was first in my line-up of holiday family flicks, despite my reservations that it held more than its share of adult humor.

I cringed a little, glancing at my kids' glowing faces, knowing the bawdy line the actress was about to deliver was too crude for young ears. It was a mother's job to filter out the filth—at least, that's what Mom thought. That's why I'd grown up watching *It's a Wonderful Life* and *A Charlie Brown Christmas*. George Bailey and Charlie were acceptable viewing.

As my less acceptable movie rolled, I reddened at the whine from the young character Audrey about her sacrifice of bunking with her little brother to accommodate her grandparent's sleeping arrangements. "I have nightmares about what he does in his bed alone when I'm not lying right next to him." Leave it to the daughter to speak her truth.

I could relate to Christmas's high personal costs. It was true. For the entire family to be happy during the holidays, someone had to suffer. Ellen, the movie mom, summed it up better than I ever could. "Well, I don't know what to say, except it's Christmas, and we're all in misery." The camera cut to a head of lettuce on the chopping block, which Ellen executed with one swift blow of a cleaver. Leave it to the mother to cut straight to the absolute truth.

Like Ellen, I was miserable. Bitterness seeped in while I tromped through slushy store parking lots in search of joy for someone else. I should've never given in to the lie. Jesus was the reason for the season, but I'd caved to Santa. Jesus came as a peaceful babe, Santa with a flood of anxiety. You'd think it would change after the kids got older.

But I had a mom who'd set the bar a whole notch higher than Santa.

* * *

Christmas excitement blasted through the first-grade classroom like the hot air cranking from the register. My friends rattled off their lengthy Christmas lists. Then it was my turn. "An EZ-Bake oven, a Spirograph, Dancerina, Winnie the Pooh—"

"There's no Santa," hissed a wiser first grader who happened to have older brothers. "It's your mom and dad." She sat back and smiled, quite pleased at disrupting my dream.

Devastated, I ran home to report the lie to Mom, who gave Dad a funny, frozen glance. "Honey, that's not true. There is a Santa." I wanted to believe her, but the evidence against the real Santa was mounting.

"I wonder what Santa's going to bring Mommy for Christmas?" Dad asked when he tucked me in that night, peeking over his shoulder at her silhouette in the doorway.

"Nothing, Warren!" she scolded, dropping her tone to a loud whisper that roared in my ears. "You know we can't afford much this year."

The next day, while Mom clipped coupons, I shortened my list. "I'm asking Santa for a Dancerina doll," I announced.

Mom looked up with a little frown, then a smile. "Anything else?"

"That's all I want," I said, running off before she spotted the lie.

On Christmas morning, I anxiously descended the stairs to discover a mountain of perfectly wrapped joy under the tree. One by one, I opened every single present I'd dreamed of and more. How did Santa know? I never asked him!

The true joy of Christmas came from sacrifice, but Mom led me to believe it was magic.

* * *

We were due at Mom and Dad's in an hour for our annual gift exchange, a sometimes painful, usually awkward gathering where we pretended nothing had changed since the days of Pooh and Dancerina. Mom could be expected to rise to the occasion as usual, gifting each of us with the one item we desperately needed but had no idea that we did until she placed it in our hands.

Once I'd become a mom, the effort behind the dreamy Christmas family portrait of my childhood had slowly come into focus. Mom had given so much over the years, never expecting anything in return. How do you outgive the gift giver herself? The question had me tied up in knots. This year, none of us needed a single thing, but all of us wanted the same present. We wanted Jesus to heal Mom so the celebrations could continue.

I swallowed the lump in my throat, grabbed the overstuffed shirt box containing a sweater for Mom, and got to work. Silver shears sliced through paper I then folded, pulled taut, and taped to cover up a present that would join the others never a surprise to Mom.

"Oh!" she'd exclaim. "A blue sweater! It's beautiful!" I imagined her storing the gift later that night, atop a growing pile of exact replicas from Christmases gone by.

I pushed the scene from my mind, unraveled a spool of green curling ribbon, made and applied a few curls, and then stepped back to consider my work. Cute, but not enough. I unraveled a little more, then more, snipping one piece after another, weaving it through the others until I'd created a mountain of curly green Christmas love for Mom to behold. It was hideous.

Chuck peeked in the front door. "Ready to go?"

"Ready as I'll ever be."

* * *

After scarfing down the honey-baked ham and scalloped potatoes, we tossed the paper plates into the garbage and filed into the living room to gather by the tree. "We should have dined on real plates," Mom said, gathering up the leftovers with a forlorn look.

"Lynn, it's fine!" Dad assured her, shooing her out of the kitchen. That was their way. He talked her into making things easier, and she later regretted agreeing to the shortcut. After a lifetime of watching them say the same lines over and over, I could predict what came next.

"Well, next Christmas, we're dining on china!" Nobody challenged Mom, especially now.

Her face held a mixture of emotions: joy at the surprise visit by her youngest child and his wife, elation at having us all in one room, and the unspoken grief that this Christmas could be the last. Not one person spoke of her swollen cheeks or the wig that framed them. It was business as usual.

Mom sat near the tree, directing Dad in gift distribution. "This one's for Kati. Oh, this one, too. Here's Chapin's. Chapin's. Kati, Kati, Chapin. Where's the other one for Chapin? Warren? Do you see it?"

"No, Lynn. How am I supposed to see anything with all this

paper?"

"It's OK, Dad, Mom. It'll turn up." I winked at both kids, and they grinned. They knew how this scenario played out, too.

Mom got up to search through the remaining pile. "It's here. I know I put it under here." Mom went through the presents a second time, then sat back down, defeated.

"It's OK, Nanny," Chapin said.

"Well, if we can't find it . . . ." Mom's voice trailed off, leaving an uncomfortable gap in the conversation. To my recollection, she'd never lost anything, until now.

In the background, Judy Garland crooned "Have Yourself a Merry Little Christmas," a song I loved. But there was a phrase I took issue with, especially now. Over the smooth words "if the fates allow," I softly sang the truth. "If *God* allows." I waved my arms to make a little show of it. "C'mon, everyone! You know the words."

"You know the words, sis." Josh's eyes sparkled with mischief. "But should you *sing* them?" I let the insult slide. He was right. I couldn't hold a note to save my life, but I'd hold one as long as necessary if it could save Mom's.

At the candlelight service later that night, Mom and I climbed up the church steps together, arm in arm, more to steady her gait than mine. Entering the toasty foyer, I stomped the snow off my boots, then went to help with her coat.

"Hey, nice sweater!"

"Well, you got it for me."

"Yeah, guess I got good taste, huh?"

I stepped back to admire my gift selection. The sweater hugged her torso a little too tightly, but she had expertly balanced it out with a flared wool skirt. I kicked myself. I didn't think about how much cancer had drastically changed the shape of our lives, hers most of all.

The usher handed each arrival a candle and the same recurring joke. "I heard it's so cold Santa's staying home tonight." Chuckling, he indicated the route to the candlelight service with a tip of his head.

I laughed, but not at the joke. After all these years, no one had to direct Mom and me toward the sanctuary. It was the same building with different people walking the same worn carpeted aisle. We both knew the path by heart.

The church was filling up fast. "If Santa changes his mind, he better hurry," I said, claiming the last empty row close to the front. "Let's spread out," I advised to accommodate our family stragglers. Usually, the only straggler was me. But this year was different. I didn't want to miss anything.

The low lighting made Mom and me whisper and communicate in silly sign language from across the pew. We were saying the identical thing but with our unique gestures. *Save a spot for the kids.*

Christmas was all about kids—the kids we raised and loved and the kids we once were. The music started; I tried not to panic. My children would find their way.

Kids always do, right? One glance at Mom told me that she'd never stopped believing. Moms never do. I followed her eyes to a makeshift manger set on the stage, the ancient prop stored behind the baptismal tank year after year, dusted off for another retelling of the Savior's birth. My children had outgrown the Christmas pageant the manger awaited, but the memories were fresh in my mind.

* * *

Kati was to play an angel. The irony was not lost on me.

"Sit still! Just gotta pin this wing."

"OUCH!!!! Mom! You HURT me!!!" The drama turned a few heads backstage. Why had this child not received the starring role?

"Sorry. But I need you to NOT move until I get this." Talking around the razor-sharp pins held handy in my teeth was a feat. How had Mom managed?

With one more tug on each end of the drapery cord around my daughter's tiny waist, I pulled the costume all together. "There!" I declared. "You're an angel." I went off in search of the Little Drummer Boy. I never had to worry if Kati knew her lines or where to stand. My only concern was that she remembered I was there.

But six-year-old Chapin's responsibility, his first solo, applied too much pressure on both of us. I knelt to look him in the eyes, adjusting his scratchy shepherd's tunic while I encouraged him for his big stage debut. Coaching him on singing was as ironic as preparing his sister to be an angel. Sometimes, mothers don't get to pick the roles they're asked to play. We wing it, say a prayer, and hope for the best.

Though I didn't have a part in the play, I had the jitters, not nervous for me but anxious for them. I wanted them to enjoy what little time they had on the stage, to do their best and know it was perfect to me.

I slipped into the pew between Mom and Chuck as the spotlight captured three angelic beings poised by the grand piano, ready to announce the coming of Christ. "Behold, I bring you good tidings of great joy."[18] Great joy was the feeling that filled me each time my daughter took the stage and stood firmly on her mark. Had she ever wobbled, I may have run up and steadied her. She spoke on cue and sang on key. If I hadn't known better, I would've guessed she had a mother who made her practice her lines. I was the first and last to applaud my angel girl as she solemnly exited stage left.

After a brief, unplanned intermission caused by one of the stable hands, the sound of a distant drum began to beat from near

---

[18] Luke 2:10 (KJV).

the back pew. Heads swiveled to see a blue-eyed Little Drummer Boy walking down the aisle alone. My heart pounded louder than the toy drum that hung securely around his neck by Chuck's guitar strap.

Our son stopped at the microphone, and the actors repositioned. My eyes were trained on him except for the brief second that I closed them to send up a last-minute prayer. *Please, God. Help him.*

Chapin's low, raspy voice rang clear and true through the air, sweet to my ears. He didn't miss a single word. His face, so young and serious, made me pause at the words he sang. If all we had to lay before the King was our pauper hearts, was that enough? I hoped so; it sure didn't feel like it to me most days.

The passing of time hadn't improved my odds either. The chances of me ever becoming good enough to stand before the King ran neck and neck with the immaculate conception. But come to think of it, Mary didn't make that impossibility happen; God did.

* * *

Pastor Tom struck the familiar chord that interrupted my thoughts and ushered in a crowd favorite, "Mary, Did You Know?"

Did Mary know? That was a good question. She could explain who, what, why, and when, but not how. As a soon-to-be teen mom, she readily agreed to accept the role of unwed mother in a society that stoned women for it. Mary's problems were much more significant than buying the right present or pulling the turkey out of the oven in time. Yet she chose a selfless life over a selfish one, ushering in the first Christmas with a resounding YES, not a mediocre *meh*.

That sacrifice brought Mary face-to-face with God in the flesh, so close she pressed her lips to His face. I couldn't imagine feeling that close to Jesus, but Mom's look as the song ended told me she could.

When I got home, I popped in an old home movie from Christmas past to see if I could find the joy missing in my Christmas present. What I saw confirmed my suspicions.

Viewing the film was like watching a movie on an airplane during turbulence. Scenes cut in and out, angles changed, but the cinematography was priceless, retelling the story of a childhood chapter I knew by heart.

* * *

Josh's grin stretched his chubby cheeks to their limits as he and I jumped up and down in our pajamas. We danced around evergreen branches weighed down with tinsel and surrounded by stacks of brightly wrapped boxes topped with tidy bows.

Mom sat nearby on the shag carpet, her back to the camera. Even before dawn, she was impeccably dressed in a stylish burgundy jumper, her hair shiny and curled over a crisp-collared shirt.

Dad made it his quest to capture her beauty that Christmas morning, but no matter how many times he circled, she turned away at the last minute.

He must have grown tired of the chase and decided to pan out to the perimeters of the joyous Christmas scene, revealing actors I didn't remember being there. Grandma? Uncle Donnie and Uncle Henry?

The interruption in a previously viewed episode of my life confused me. I tried to recall details but was forced to sit back and observe as the camera continued to roll.

Mom's two brothers sported thick, handsome sideburns and unreadable faces, one holding up a tennis racket and the other a book, no doubt carefully selected gifts from their sister. Grandma sat in an armchair across the room, holding a cigarette in one hand and opening a gift box with the other, its contents spilling over into her lap. She showed the silky blouse to the camera with a slow smile, accentuated by hastily applied red lipstick. She raised a hand to shield the glaring camera light, but it reflected orbs from her cloudy eyes.

Mom sat at Grandma's feet, her face turned away from the camera and toward her mother, whose legs were sprawled in an unladylike fashion, covered by knee socks that barely reached their destination and rubber boots that swallowed her feet.

In filmmaking, timing is crucial. As if on cue, Dad's lens finally hit its intended target, zooming in on Mom's exquisite stricken face at the exact same time her heart was rejected by her mother's for the twenty-ninth Christmas in a row.

The contrast between the two women was striking—Grandma unkempt and oblivious to the pain she caused, Mom physically pulled together and emotionally hanging on by a thread. Somehow, Mom had repeatedly wrapped up her sadness and tucked it under the tree, where it mysteriously turned into joy for my brother and me every Christmas morning.

* * *

I wanted to call her, but it was too late, and I didn't know how to express my gratitude.

A mother's sacrifice can bring both misery and joy. How you choose to wrap it determines what your kids open in the end.

I learned that from her.

Chapter 9

Needle and Thread

"Mom! Costumes came in!" Kati dropped bags on the table and ran off to finish her homework. Time moved too fast. Though winter had barely melted into spring, the arrival of recital costumes announced summer was officially on its way. One season quickly slipped into the next without warning.

Like Michigan weather, Mom's illness also experienced sudden changes, some as pleasant as the sight of the apple trees in blossom. "The doctor says I'm cancer-free!"

Just as quickly, a tornado was spotted on the horizon, wreaking havoc on the beauty of the first sign of spring, strewing its petals and branches across the lawn. "The cancer's back and spreading. They want to treat it with a stronger drug."

The weaker Mom got, the less she appeared to desire company, so I trained my focus on my immediate family. While I reviewed carpool schedules, I mentally inserted Mom's treatments in my calendar, wondering if my presence would be wanted. Did she really wish to be alone? Or was she only saying that to keep from being a burden? Over the phone, her weary voice provided few clues.

Chuck walked in after our daughter, dumping a stack of mail

next to the costume bags. "Recital time, huh? How many dances this year?"

"Can't remember. Five? Six?" I sorted through the labeled baggies, deciphering each costume's needs. Like life, costumes didn't come fully assembled. Extra work was required.

Sewing didn't come naturally to me. I loathed threading a needle almost as much as asking Mom to help thread it. Through the years, I employed Chuck's help when I could, like the night I asked him to sew a patch on Kati's Brownie vest.

"I know it's late, but the glue gun's not cutting it this time."

"Sure," he said. "You know, I got an A in Bachelor Living."

"Yes, I know. Good for you. I bet your teacher adored you."

My Home Ec teacher hated me. The last day before my sewing project was due, she ripped the seams out of my apron and handed it back to me in a heap of frayed denim.

"This has to be redone if you want to pass," she said.

I'd taken it to Mom in tears. She attempted to work a miracle, but my handiwork sins were not redeemed. I'd botched it good this time. Because the fabric store was closed, she couldn't whip up another apron, so she did the best repair possible. Neither of us addressed that we were tossing our closely held Christian ethics and souls out the window to save our reputations. Submitting her work as mine was a desperate act for desperate times.

I hid the D- on my report card from her as long as possible. I didn't know which was worse, hiding the truth or seeing the look of shame on her face when I handed it over.

"Be sure your sin will find you out,"[19] she often warned me, and my having a dancing daughter provided living proof.

For the first three years of Kati's dance career, I swallowed my pride and asked for Mom's help with the dance costumes. Three

---

[19] Numbers 32:23 (NKJV).

years of depending on her felt like losing a lifetime of independent ground. For three years, I watched over her shoulder as she made quick, neat stitches I was incapable of, while I felt like I didn't have what it took to be a mom.

After three years, I decided I'd learn to sew if it killed me, and I thought it just might. Mom's old sewing machine and two yards of cornflower-blue calico sneered at me from across the room.

"Honey, I'd be happy to show you," Mom had offered.

"Nope, I'll figure it out," I snipped. I could teach myself.

The thought of being under Mom's scrutiny for hours on end was too high a price to pay for a skill that looked simple to acquire once I was older and wiser. Besides, how long had I stood in the doorway of her sewing room as a child and observed? She made it look easy, clipping, pinning, and guiding fabric through her whirring Singer.

My optimism was short-lived. As soon as I pulled the so-called EZ Sew dress pattern out of its jacket, I forgot everything Mom taught me about naming and claiming victory. *Nikki, you are an idiot.*

Stubbornly, I pressed ahead for hours, mimicking Mom's seamstress moves from a faulty memory, digging uneven stitches out with a seam ripper and a vengeance, angry at myself for running out the door to play as a little girl instead of sitting at my mother's feet. The pattern tissue tore, my cuts were jagged, and the fabric puckered under the machine's foot, creating a monstrosity meant to be a smock.

When I held the pitiful version of a little girl's dress up to waning light with pinpricked, bleeding fingers, I declared the garment unfit to wipe the floor, let alone be worn by my daughter. I threw the rag in the trash and sold the Singer at the next garage sale. It was a humbling experience with a lesson learned: I was destined to be at Mom's mercy for the rest of my days as a dance mom.

The assembly maneuvers required by the latest costumes were

more than daunting. Unfortunately, sewing sequins on flimsy fabric wasn't part of Chuck's Bachelor Living curriculum or in my DNA. My only option was to ask for Mom's help.

Lately, though, I'd begun to feel convicted about my "good daughter" grade. I deserved a D-. I should probably pop over and see how I could help Mom before asking for another sewing miracle.

I'd keep Kati's costumes in the car, just in case I got the green light. If Mom couldn't help, maybe she could guide this fumbling-fingered daughter of hers. Much like a rich person entering Heaven through the eye of a needle[20] my sewing skills had been labeled impossible to save. Jesus said such impossibilities required divine intervention.

Before I dialed Mom's number, the phone rang in my hand.

"Mom? I was just getting ready to call you!"

"Hi, honey." It was Dad.

"Oh, ha! Thought you were—"

"We're on our way to the hospital. The doctor thinks Mom's port is infected. I'll call you in the morning and let you know how she's doing."

Panic seized me. I was too late. I should've barged in and checked on Mom regardless of any protest. All the excuses I'd used to avoid her sounded lame. It was time for action.

I'd barely hung up when I rerouted our weekend plans. "Kids, we're going to visit Nanny in the morning." I turned to my husband. "You in?" He nodded. Might as well make it a family affair.

The following morning, we loaded the car for a visit. It didn't occur to me to call first. Even if it had, I'd have argued against such precaution as part of the flawed mindset that had prevented me from visiting her as much as I should've in the first place. Besides,

---

[20] Matthew 19:24 (KJV).

I was bringing her grandkids, the best medicine ever.

Stepping off the elevator, I had a funny feeling. *Why'd Dad say he'd call me, rather than tell me to come right away?*

Overthinking didn't get anyone anywhere. I pushed the qualm aside and proceeded with what I knew, not what I didn't. The commonly held belief was that a good daughter visits her mother in the hospital, so I was confident I was headed in the right direction.

I approached Mom's hospital room with caution, lightly rapping on the door. When the kids ran past and burst in, I hurried to catch up, toting sunshine, smiles, and a bouquet of flowers.

"Hey, Mom! Look who came to see you!"

Mom's ice-water glare abruptly doused our enthusiasm. To my surprise, the flowers didn't wilt, and neither did I. But I realized I hadn't taken into account that my mother might be hanging on by an emotional thread.

"Nanny!" The kids charged to her bedside for their usual warm hug, only to scurry back, rebuffed by her frigid shoulder.

Seeing their hurt and confusion plunged a seam ripper into my heart. This wasn't the grandma they knew, but it was the mother I'd become acquainted with on and off throughout my life. I'd learned to try to ignore her rude behavior.

"Um, how ya doin', Mom? What'd the doctor say?" My effort at conversation offered the only bit of grace I could muster.

Like a child, she turned her head without replying. Silence was her weapon of choice when backed into a corner. You'd think its effect would have dulled after years of having it wielded against me. But the blade proved sharp as ever, ripping out the delicate threads that held me together, methodically dismantling me one stitch at a time.

I'd almost have preferred cutting words to her indifference. At least words would provide clues to what we'd done wrong. Her continued silence left me guessing. Maybe my efforts were too little too late. Maybe my presence was too much. Maybe I'd never know how to fix myself to make her love me and my family how we needed to be loved. Maybe my only fault was that I kept trying.

Chuck read the situation and intervened, steering our confused herd from the room. "Nice to see you, Lynn," he called over his shoulder. "Hope you feel better soon."

As the elevator doors shut behind us, I berated myself for having high expectations. Now, there was another impossible situation to mend. In my limited sewing experience, hurt feelings between two offended parties were the most challenging gap to repair.

* * *

Sande, my best friend, leaned to whisper discreetly in my ear. "I think you're leaking."

"Oh!" I adjusted my newborn son to cover the wet spot on my blouse and continued opening gifts with one hand. My mother-in-law, Barb, had insisted on throwing me a baby shower because five years had passed since my last one. She was eager to help.

"Nikki, give me that baby!" she cried. At my reluctance, she teased me with a smile and short, quick shakes of her head. "I know how to hold a baby." She'd had four before the age of twenty-three. Compared to me, overwhelmed by two children, she was the expert.

Still, I shook my head, refusing to put another burden in her lap. "I'm OK." I moved my son from one arm to another.

But I wasn't OK. I was shaking, exhausted, sweating, and sore. The only woman I'd readily accept help from was sitting across the room in a corner booth, sipping coffee with her passel of friends and not giving me the time of day. The reason I deduced for the snub was unfair, especially since I'd made an effort to do everything right this time around.

When I went into labor, I called to let Mom know. "Please,

come up. You and Barb can sit in the waiting room. As soon as the baby's born, come in." Exactly four hours later, I'd presented my son to Chuck and then to Mom.

"He's perfect, honey," she said. "Look at all that hair! Kati's going to have so much fun being a big sister. What's his name?"

"Chapin Niles," Chuck announced proudly, stepping into the conversation from behind.

I swallowed hard, reading Mom's fallen face. I had hoped to break the news to her more gently. Chapin was named after Chuck's beloved Grandpa Chapin, who'd recently passed. *Niles* was a middle name the other side of Chuck's family had passed down through generations. Now that Chuck said the name aloud in her presence, it felt like my family of origin was left in the dust.

I'd been musing over girls' names for nine months, not knowing Chapin was a boy. Before Kati was born, I did the opposite, selecting the name *Charles Warren*. Five years had passed, but Mom must have assumed *Charles Warren* was still in the running. My dad was most likely passing out bubble gum cigars in the waiting room to honor his namesake.

Mom left the hospital somewhat abruptly after our son's name was revealed. No one else thought much of it, but I knew her exit indicated trouble.

Was it my fault I wasn't close with my extended family like Chuck? Mom wasn't around to answer that question. After I came home from the hospital, she remained mysteriously unavailable. When she accepted the shower invite, I was surprised and assumed she'd done so to keep up appearances. But she made it very clear that I'd crossed a line. I'd chosen Chuck over Mom again.

The more the other shower attendees celebrated my adorable blue-eyed boy, the heavier the silent judgment from the corner booth felt, causing my turbulent hormones to boil. In a barely contained rage, I held up a gift.

"Mom?" I called syrupy sweet. "Mom! Look at this cute outfit for your grandson. Isn't it adorable?"

The question called everyone's attention to the stone-faced woman no one would've suspected to be the baby's grandma. What I wanted to ask her was different. *Do you see me struggling over here? Why can't you forgive me for being less than perfect? Your blessing is the only gift I've ever wanted. I know I don't deserve it, but can I have it? Pretty please?*

The eyes zeroed in on her forced her to respond. "Yes, very cute," she said in a clipped tone, hiding her real feelings behind the coffee cup she held in a death grip. The way her sisters in Christ leaned in closer around her as if she were the one under attack reopened old wounds I thought were healed.

When the torture of the event was over, Mom and her friends slipped out with a few quick goodbyes. I hefted a diaper bag in one arm, a baby carrier in the other, and looked over my shoulder, making sure Kati followed close behind. Barb and her friends were busy taking down decorations and promised to deliver and unpack the stack of gifts after I settled in back home.

As soon as I entered the parking lot, I encountered Mom, still snubbing me, and I felt engulfed in a silent hurricane of the emotions she managed to keep at bay. I fought to appear calm and unaffected, turning away to secure my children in the car. As I buckled the car seats, I prayed a half-crazed declaration of faith. *I will not engage. I will not engage.* In the middle of my chant, I snapped anyway, whirled around, and marched into the storm. Mom turned pale as a ghost. Her friends' mouths dropped open as I came face-to-face with the woman who'd rejected and humiliated me publicly. Not once did I consider that she may have felt the same way.

"You know, Mom. If you're going to make me choose, I choose my husband. I'll choose him every time."

She flinched as if I'd struck her, but what did she expect? As far as I was concerned, I owed her no apology for my son's name. I waited for my hands to stop shaking before I put the car in reverse. Her car pulled out of the parking lot first, turning right, so I turned left. We drove in opposite directions for over a month.

Banished from her presence, part of me refused to believe that a mother, let alone a grandmother, could be so cold and unforgiving. Whenever I heard a car door slam while I was in the house, I ran to the window, then reluctantly returned to nursing my growing son without her blessing. Pride was horrible company. I wanted my Mom.

* * *

Following the unwanted hospital visit, raw feelings of the past returned. After I'd worked so hard to baste my heart to Mom's, one impulsive move had ripped the effort to shreds. Our relationship was frayed at the edges again, possibly beyond hope of repair.

I rolled the sequins for a costume between my fingers, considering how to approach a task I had little natural skill for. Why did dancers insist on wearing fancy, elaborate getups for one fleeting dance? Why don't costumes arrive fully assembled, ready to go? Not requiring teamwork would make life easier—but perhaps lonelier, too.

Out of the blue, I recalled the secret thread that mended the rift between Mom and me after that baby shower a decade ago. We had a mutual, relentless desire to see my children, her grandchildren, grow up and thrive. Before I lost courage, I dialed her number.

"Hi, Mom. It's me. Could I come over? I need help with Kati's costumes. Only if you're up to it, of course." To my relief, Mom agreed.

Still, since I didn't know if our relationship was yet out of the woods of disappointment, I went alone. I entered the house cautiously, afraid of what mood I'd find.

"Hello?"

"In here." Mom's voice was almost inaudible from where she sat at the round oak table, sorting through a thread collection, pincushion ready on her wrist. She glanced up with puffy eyes and offered a limp smile before returning to organizing her tools.

I greeted her with a quick, awkward hug equivalent to embracing a marble statue, then winced when the chair I pulled out screeched in protest. Carefully, I laid the most challenging costume of the season on the table. It was vulnerable to snags and much too delicate for rough handling. There was no doubt I'd come to the right place to complete its transformation. Mom had the skills needed to make the costume whole.

Her fingers busied themselves with thread, her jaw set firm. I was at her mercy and no longer cared to pretend I wasn't. Life was short; I needed her beside me.

"Mom, I'm sorry. I shouldn't have surprised you at the hospital like that. I should've checked to see if you wanted visitors. Will you forgive me?" The dam of tears I'd held burst before my plea was out.

Her face registered no emotion. She looked down and cleared her throat as if considering what to say. "You know, I once read that the most spiritually mature person apologizes first."

Stunned at the compliment, I said nothing. She looked up and smiled. "And here you are." After a pause, she added "I'm sorry, too, honey." Her lips parted to say more, but she pulled the thread container to her instead. "Now, how many costumes must we assemble for Miss Kati Marie?"

"Um, *we*?" I said shakily. Her laugh told me all was forgiven and that you're never too old to learn. Lord knows you should never stop trying.

Gifted with quick and efficient fingers, Mom wasted no time assembling the costumes using minute, even stitches. Out of respect, I watched for a while, threading together a string of family news and events that she'd missed during our time apart. After all safe subjects of conversation were exhausted, I made myself useful by washing the few dishes in the sink and daydreaming out the window.

"Mom?"

"Hmm?"

"You guys took the sandbox out?" Maybe it had been gone a while, but I hadn't noticed.

"Yes." Mom lowered her hands and rested them on the table, holding the fabric taut and looking at me with eyes that had accepted the inevitable. "It was time."

I dried my hands on the dish towel, considering her words. The passing of time was one thing that couldn't be fixed. I learned that from her.

"They're growing up on us, aren't they?"

We were all growing up together.

Chapter 10

Accept No Imitation

September arrived on cue without one idea for a suitable birthday gift for Mom. My expectations were low; it only had to be better than last year's gift.

"Oh, what's this?" Mom had said when I handed her *Healing Traumatic Childhood Wounds*. "I haven't heard of this book."

"It came highly recommended at the Christian bookstore. I thought . . ." *What was I thinking again?* My face burned.

"That's so sweet, honey. But I'm not sure why you gave me this. I had a wonderful childhood." Mom stared into space with an odd, dreamy look.

Had I misread random oddities that I thought were clues?

She informed us that firefly wings tasted like potato chips, and pigeons made great pets She expertly ducked out of all male hugs, taking two paces back.

I longed to solve the mystery of why the closer I got to Mom, the farther away I felt. As usual, when it came to understanding Mom, I was wrong.

"I'll return it and get something you want," I said last year. *Maybe a new daughter?*

This year, her birthday made more precious by cancer, I'd wracked my brain for months but was down to days to come up with a gift. In an uncharacteristic, decisive move, I marched into the jewelry store and pointed to a string of pearls.

"How much are those?" Wincing at the clerk's reply, I moved slightly to the right. "What about those? The freshwater ones." The beads weren't as smooth but boasted the pearls label without the hefty price tag.

Would Mom even know the cost I was willing to pay to make her smile? What if I bought the pearls and she hated them? All that money would be wasted in a futile attempt at winning her affection once and for all. But time was short, leaving me little choice.

"I'll take them," I decided. Perhaps they'd eventually come back to me, and I could pass them down to Kati. *What kind of person thinks like that?* It was hard to careen between the realities of Mom living or dying. Nothing could soften the latter reality, not even a string of cultured pearls.

Doubt accompanied me into a restaurant booth later that afternoon, as doubt often did with any decision involving her. I'd chosen one of Mom's favorite restaurants, where she could order a good steak.

"My treat!" I'd insisted, sensing her hesitation. Alternative medicine treatments were clawing through my parents' collective wallet.

The server took our orders, beginning with the birthday girl.

"I'll just have water for now, thank you." Mom frowned and swallowed, holding her hand to her throat.

"Aren't you hungry, Mom?" She answered my stupid question with a slight shake of her head while the server continued around the table. "Then I'll just have a salad." It didn't seem right to gobble down a steak in front of her. It didn't feel right to enjoy life at all when hers was so hard.

The food arrived, and everyone but Mom dug in. I shoveled forkfuls of salad into my big mouth. Mom sipped her water like poison. I almost forgot it was a celebration, until the server rounded the corner with a piece of cake, a blazing candle, and a much-too-peppy rendition of the birthday song.

"Happy birthday, dear Mom." My singing was off-key like usual, sounding more like a dirge. Even with the candlelight dancing across her face, her complexion and mood were lackluster.

Picking up the pace to match the servers' voices, we raced to the end of an uncomfortable moment. Normally, my favorite part of the birthday song was taking the good wishes up another notch with the encore line, pushing the last note of "And many more" to my lung's limit, exhaling all of me into the recipient's years as if I had the power to increase their longevity with my breath.

Death and life are in the power of the tongue.[21] I'd been taught that Bible verse early in life, and I wrestled with it now. If I sang to declare many more years over Mom's life, would I be acting in denial of where that life was headed? No one knew the future or how long a person's life would be. Our tongues had the power of life and death, but only Jesus Christ held the keys.

As usual, I settled on a compromise, making two definitive claps that could be interpreted as people wished, then pushing the gift toward her. "For you! Happy birthday, Mom!"

Unexpected tears sprung to my eyes, and I pretended to look through my purse for a tissue. Mom waited for me to finish the unsuccessful search and smiled weakly, slowly opening the card.

"You don't have to read it right now," I said, waving my hand toward the real, wrapped gift. I had hoped for the most appropriate words to flow onto the card, but the ink had smeared, and the celebratory words didn't make sense anymore. We were all going

[21] Proverbs 18:21 (KJV).

through the motions in a trance to protect ourselves from the pain of having little power to control what happened next.

Mom broke open the package seal with her finger.

"You can take it back if you don't like it," I blurted.

I'd sworn I wouldn't say the same line she offered with every gift she gave, as if what she had to give wasn't good enough, right enough, or plain enough to satisfy the recipient. But I was weak with grief, and the apple didn't fall far from the tree. Able to quote the script by heart, I continued with the next line. "I won't be offended. Really."

How could one not be offended when a gift is refused? But I meant it whether I said it to Mom or anyone else. I wanted the other person to be happy and at liberty to return the item to get something wanted. That was how you showed someone your love.

I learned that from her.

I couldn't read Mom's face when she opened the box. As if reading my thoughts, she smiled politely and held up the pearls so everyone could ooh and aah.

"Do you like them?" I jumped into the pool of potential rejection with both feet, wanting to get the sting of Mom's inevitable reaction over with. Her enthusiasm rarely met mine.

Other questions lay buried in my four words. *Do you like me? Do you wish you could return me? Am I enough? Am I everything you ever hoped to receive?*

"Yes, thank you." The polite response was the best she could offer. She set the lid back on the box and set it aside. "You shouldn't have. It's too much."

She was referring to the pearls, but I read her words to mean me. I was too much. Initially weighing in at eight pounds and two ounces, I was more than she could bear.

I looked away and signaled the server. "Check, please? We better go, Mom, and let you get some rest. The kids have school tomorrow, too." I hugged her goodbye, careful not to squeeze too hard or too long. It was the day before she turned fifty-nine, and I didn't want to put any more pressure on her than I already had.

In the following weeks, I popped by every few days to say hi and see what I could do for her around the house. Doing for her was less painful than sitting with her. If I sat still too long, it'd be painfully apparent there was nothing more either of us could do to move closer. One of us might say something we'd regret and push the other farther away.

During one visit, Mom lay on the couch, facing the TV. Dad clicked on her favorite soap opera, propped her up with pillows, and covered her with an afghan, taking care not to move too fast. She was like a piece of broken china glued together but not fully intact. From afar, one would think her a woman of leisure, choosing to gift herself a well-deserved break. Up close, you could see the thin gauze that held her wounded hope together unraveling.

I preferred a safe distance, so I could imagine her as she once was, twirling around the room with her grandbabies, scooping up ice cream for dinner, making up silly dances for hours until she fell exhausted and satisfied on the couch. That was the woman I missed most, the mom I wished I had the chance to know better.

Dad headed out to mow the lawn. "Need anything?" When Mom shook her head, he was dismissed. "Then I'll leave you girls alone." The pictures on the fireplace mantle shook when he closed the door behind him.

I stood with a feather duster in one hand, a rag in the other, and a cleaning bucket suspended on my right arm, all reminding me why I came. I checked my watch. There was little time to chat, but focusing on cleaning would leave Mom alone. Why was it so hard to stop doing and just be? Out of obligation, I perched on the edge of the room's armchair, ready to spring back into action should Dad return to keep her company.

Mom turned to me with great effort. She winced and smiled, rubbing her forearm with a black-and-blue hand. "How're the kids?" she asked, pretending all was well by carrying on an everyday ordinary conversation.

"Good. They're good." My stare fixed on her arm. "Does your arm hurt?" There, I'd said it. I hoped she'd forgive me for not playing along.

She waited to answer, as if she thought I might run out and report the truth to Dad. But something about me must've looked trustworthy. "A little," she confessed. "Starting last night. Must've slept on it funny."

"Huh." An alarm sounded inside, but I'd been schooled in the prosperity gospel that taught that one negative word could spark a fire of doubt that burned your entire testimony down.

She looked off into some faraway place where throbbing arms were cured. I couldn't make her pain go away, but I had to do something for her, even if my efforts were futile. "Need anything? Another blanket?" She responded with one deep inhale, then a sputtering exhale. My arm began to ache like my heart.

Dad burst through the door. "I can't believe that guy did it again!"

Mom grimaced and pushed herself up to face him. Harsh lines that etched her forehead a second before melted. Gritted teeth flashed a brilliant smile. I was stunned by her sudden transformation from personal agony to concerned, devoted wife. This woman whose discomfort I had been able to read like a book was going for Oscar gold.

"What guy, honey? What'd he do?"

Dad launched into a tirade about the mailman delivering a package to the wrong address. Her eyes never leaving his face, she spurred him on with sympathetic nods and murmurs. There was no mention of the pain wrongly delivered to her, only concern that Dad was inconvenienced.

I once thought Dad was the stronger of my parents. No matter how hard his day was or how weary his shoulders, he entered Mom's world eager to serve.

"Now Lynn, you rest," he used to say after coming home from work to a wife too overwhelmed by the day's highs and lows to make the family dinner. He'd take the heap of dirty laundry out of her arms and escort her to the couch, insisting she put her feet up because the load was too heavy for her to carry. I grew to resent her weak, halfhearted protests as he pulled the shades and laid a cool washcloth on her forehead. Rings of sweat stained his work shirt as he ran the heavy Hoover back and forth while she watched in shame. I was ashamed of her weakness and vowed to be more like Dad.

Now, their roles had reversed in an odd twist of cancerous fate. She was Dad's protector from an evil mailman; Dad, the weaker sex. Despite her brave mask, the truth was written all over her face. She was losing the battle. The mail carrier pulled back in the driveway, and Dad happily went out to meet him. Mom's facade disappeared.

Unsure how to respond to what I'd witnessed, I returned to my task. The fireplace mantle was thick with dust and crowded with pictures, an excellent place to start. Mom had begun to spend most of her time in this room, so it should be kept up to her impeccable standards.

I pulled down the photo frames, wiped the glass that kept each memory safe, then ran a damp rag over the mantle. One by one, I put the photos back in line: a younger me in a prom dress, my teenage brother in a tux, our father in army fatigues, mom and dad in simple wedding attire.

Two favorite photos held center stage. The first showed Mom's head thrown back in delight—the beginning of one of her giggling fits, no doubt—while five-year-old Kati, looking quite pleased at the reaction, rested her elbows comfortably on Nanny's thigh. There was no mistaking the love between them.

The second picture framed an unhindered moment between Nanny and grandson. Mom was kneeling, eyes closed, chin lifted by a smile that displayed her pride and the rapture of wrapping her arms around Chapin, so unlike the embraces she and I shared as adults. My hand lingered on the tarnished metal frame, my heart unwilling to let go of a precious time.

But something was missing from the gallery. Eyes frantic, I spun around to locate where I'd misplaced it.

"You set it behind the TV." Mom had been watching my every move.

"Oh?" She was right again. I held up the prized picture, showing it to her. "Remember this?"

She reached out and nodded. "Let me see it."

I placed the memory in her hands, intent on her face. I knew every pore of her skin and was fluent in her body language; the lift of her brow, the quiver of her chin, and even a flare of her nostrils told me if it was better to stay or to go. The flimsy brass frame rattled against the glass, but her gaze never wavered as she beheld the picture of the two of us, a rare instance when Dad caught us off-guard. I stepped closer and looked over her shoulder.

There we were, mother and daughter, side by side, cheek to glowing cheek, eyes and smiles bright with the promise of better days ahead. Facing the camera shoulder to shoulder, one would think we saw the world the same way. People on the outside had always assumed we had.

* * *

Mom stood behind me while I adjusted my wedding veil in the mirror. "Do you like it?" I asked. She replied with a curt, tight-lipped nod. I thought she looked absolutely lovely in her knee-length periwinkle dress, a perfect backdrop for her dark, shiny hair.

"I need the bride and her mother," the photographer called over the heads of the pink bridesmaids and gray groomsmen. Thankfully, the groom was nowhere in sight. His presence would've made the entire situation more awkward.

At first, Mom appreciated Chuck courting me. After he proposed marriage, she managed to tolerate him. But she'd had enough when my plans to attend college and marry him in five years were abandoned and replaced by a ten-month wedding-planning frenzy due to one lovesick weekend apart. Little did she know that it was all my idea—the courtship, the engagement, leaving college, moving up the wedding. Of course, Chuck was a willing participant, but I was the one that pushed. I was ready to leave home long before she was ready to let me go.

Mom and I stood against the photo backdrop like we faced a firing squad rather than a stranger with a camera. Neither one of us liked being put on display.

"Wait! I asked for the mother of the bride, not the bride's younger sister!" The photographer wore a creepy smile, gawking at red-faced Mom. Comments about her youthful appearance made her ill at ease. Or was it that she didn't like looking like me?

I stiffened as the lens focused on me. "You look beautiful," Sande called from among the bridesmaids, but that statement would never be true for me until Mom believed it, too.

A flash, pop, and click captured the two of us on a roll of film that would take months to develop, in a portrait it would take a lifetime to rightly frame.

* * *

I never saw the resemblance. Mom and I had so little in common. I viewed life through blue eyes, she through hazel. I'd always bristled at the suggestion flecks of hazel appeared in mine in candlelight, but perhaps something deep within me was sending out a beacon to the innermost parts of her, hoping we'd find each other.

"We look like sisters," I admitted.

We soaked in the revelation while the mower started again in the backyard. Had Mom always known a part of me was just like her? If so, why hadn't she fought harder to prove it?

The picture drooped in Mom's hands as the old German clock gonged twice to remind me I didn't have the luxury of a daydream. There was too much left to do. All at once, I was exhausted. I hadn't been sleeping; I didn't have time for that either, not when life was on high alert.

My eyes bounced around, identifying spots I'd missed while cleaning—the baseboard in the corner, then behind the chair. I crawled like a baby from one area to another. There was no time to stand when every second counted. A chocolate smear on the back of the armchair most likely came from the kids. I jumped up, head spinning at the physical effort and the affront. I wet another rag in the sink and returned to scrub furiously, the dark spot refusing to release itself from the pink velvet. I couldn't give up. The holidays were coming. My schedule was full. I had no idea when I could get back to finish what I'd started.

I worked in a frenzy, faster and faster until the clock struck the half hour. My feather duster stopped on a dime. Time was up. I had to go and leave with unfinished business. *What an idiot!* Mom needed me, and I failed her again. I should have come earlier and made other arrangements for the kids, but I hated to depend on anyone. What if I couldn't return the favor?

"Nikki?" A gentle voice interrupted my thoughts like a whisper calling through my nightmare. I remembered that voice. "Nikki, honey. It's OK." It's uncanny how a mother's voice can cause or calm the storms that rage through us.

Her bruised arms opened wide, waiting for me to come. All the hard and heavy resentment I'd pushed between us, the impenetrable barricade erected to prevent us from touching, crumbled beneath the tender love in her eyes.

"Oh, Momma! I'm sorry. I'm so sorry." Of all the sins I'd held against her, none was as great as my trespass that refused to receive her love. *I'm so sorry for all the years I missed it, for all the times I tried to run. I'm so sorry I wasn't a good enough daughter to fix your broken heart.*

The lost little girl in me laid down alongside her. Careful not to touch her throbbing arm, I bent at an unnatural angle to claim her shoulder with my cheek.

She hummed my favorite lullaby, its melody vibrating warmth through my soul, connecting me to parts of her I'd forgotten. When she fell asleep, I rose, pulled the covers to her chin, kissed her forehead, and slipped out the door.

After the latch clicked, I picked up the tune where she'd left off. "Little ones to him belong. They are weak, but he is strong."[22] So true.

I learned that from her.

As I backed down the driveway, the rearview mirror reflected the sun into my eyes. I tilted the mirror down to get a closer look. My eyes were definitely hazel.

---

[22] "Jesus Love Me, This I Know" by Anna Bartlett Butler (1859).

Chapter 11

Pass It On

"Your mom's here!" Chuck whispered. Alarmed, I looked up from the tournament program in my hand.

Two familiar figures appeared at the entrance of the crowded gym and slowly wove toward us through a maze of metal chairs. Even through months of brutal treatments, Nanny had proven to be a tenacious cheerleader.

Of all the traits Mom and Dad possessed, showing up for their grandkids was the hallmark. Nothing could keep them away, not the blazing sun beating down on their backs, sleet raking their faces, or a weatherman's advice to stay home.

"The weatherman must not have grandchildren," Mom always concluded, scorning any obstacle to a front-row seat. Still, I was stunned to see them at the all-day volleyball conference an hour from home. The snowy roads that morning had almost been impassable, and Mom was so frail.

Ah-choo! A woman to the right foraged through her purse for a tissue.

I had one at the ready. "Bless you," I said, passing the tissue while discreetly scooting my chair away.

December flu season was in full swing. Instantly, my ears were hypertuned to the throat clearing and hacking around me. Mom shouldn't be here. What if she got sick again, got so ill she couldn't recover? Mom was forced to bring cancer along everywhere she went. It was an unwanted companion rudely staring us down, daring us not to so much as sniffle or it would whisk her away.

The volleyball match started before Mom and Dad made it to their seats. Chairs scraped as people quickly sat down. But my parents remained standing, searching for our faces in the crowd.

"Over here!" I stood and waved until the referee's whistle commanded me to sit.

Kati glared from the court. I shrugged and mouthed *Sorry*, not a fan of the volleyball rules. What was the point of coming to a game if you had to remain silent?

Like Mom, I was a born cheerleader for the children we both loved. However, after all my experience on the sidelines, I'd yet to figure out how to do it right.

* * *

Cheering for junior high wrestling wasn't what I signed up for. I thought I'd be standing under the lights on the football field, the crisp fall air blowing my skirt up while players ran off the field and gave me grateful nods that said *We couldn't do this without you, Nikki*. They would know my name because it was emblazoned across my sweater in bold felt letters.

Yet here I was, kneeling at the edge of a stinky wrestling mat, numb knees, aching back, and sweat pouring from my armpits. I'd made the B team, not the A team. Our pitiful squad had strict instructions: stay down and keep quiet. Cheering wasn't fun; it was the most brutal sport on the planet.

There were brief periods of glory between the grunts and the whistles. When our coach gave us the nod, we let loose with the one wrestling-specific cheer in the manual. "P! *Clap*. I! *Clap*. N! C*lap, clap*. Get a pin! Get a pin! Get a pin!"

When we finished, the gym was silent. No one appreciated our presence; they were embarrassed by it.

* * *

I didn't recall Mom coming to any of the matches when I cheered. Maybe she did and I don't remember. I was too focused on myself and my performance. Now I was hyperfocused on my daughter's.

Every muscle in my body tensed when the ball headed Kati's way. She was responsible for keeping the ball in the air in her designated square radius. The whole team's fate rested on her shoulders. If she missed it, the blame would land on her.

You can do this. You can do this. Jesus, help her. A prayer for a single point was probably overkill. Didn't we all want our teams to win? Maybe so, but I'd wrestle Heaven to the ground for that girl.

Mom slid into the chair next to me, her face reflecting pins-and-needles emotion as she held her granddaughter in her sight. Her lips were moving, too. All prayer warriors were on deck.

The ball floated above Kati's head. I grabbed Mom's hand and squeezed, forgetting the needle that had dug through it only the day before. I leaned forward and watched my daughter look up, take a graceful step back, raise her arms, and pop the ball to the front row. A crouched teammate was ready and met the ball in the air. Spike! Point!

She did it! So proud of my girl, I wanted to cry. I raised my fists like a big-time wrestler and shook them at the ceiling. "Nice job, Whitey!" I yelled in a low, masculine tone revived from my old cheerleading days. It sounded like I was possessed, and I was— overcome with love and gratitude for the honor of being her mom.

My eyes searched for Kati's as a sea of faces surrounded hers, so many people clawing for her attention. She must've heard me, but did she see me? Did she know the joy she brought to my heart? Did she have any idea how the light in her blue eyes sparked life in my soul? Dear God, I hoped so. It seemed my whole life depended on this crucial season when her teenaged heart had sprouted wings and hovered out of my reach. Would I miss an opportunity to connect and lose her forever? Could I raise my hands in faith and send her off on a beautiful flight? The final score of my parenting game was up in the air for now.

I turned to Mom, her pale face swallowed up by her heavy gray coat.

"Can I help take that off? It's pretty toasty in here."

"Thanks. I'm OK. Feels a little chilly."

"Chilly?" I adjusted my chair to study her. The hazel in her eyes was lost in two jet-black seas, as if her soul had pulled the curtains to shut out the pain. It was plain to see that Mom was barely hanging on, but her chin was tilted up in defiance. I didn't dare defy her now.

"Nanny!!!" Between games, Kati burst through the crowd to deliver quick hugs for everyone. Nanny's hug lingered, and my heart broke in two. Kati knew. My daughter knew I had lied to her when I told her everything would be OK.

Nanny would get better, I'd said. Life would slow down. We'd stop all the running, roll up the sleeping bags, grab our favorite movies, and camp out all day by the Christmas tree, just us girls.

I'd announced that plan a few weeks ago, speeding down the highway to dance practice. Kati had been feeling guilty that she hadn't seen her grandma, so I tried to fix it with a promise I would keep come hell or high water. But the water was rising fast.

If Kati noticed Nanny's funny stare, she chose to ignore it. Friends were calling to her, holding up milkshakes, pulling her away from her adult fans.

"You go be with your friends," Mom said, though I knew every cell in her body was screaming *Stay a little longer*.

That was the kind of love between them. Nanny didn't have to hold her grandbaby's hand anymore. She could let go and proudly watch Kati cross a street on her own. Though the precious hand-holding days were over, nothing breaks love's relentless grip on a grandma's heart.

As Kati rushed away, I overheard one of her teammates. "Kati, I wish I played as good as you." I recognized the voice, belonging to someone who sat on the bench game after game. It was as if she launched her heart toward Kati, knowing her teammate wouldn't drop it.

"Kelly! Are you serious? You're way better than me. I wish my serve was as good as yours."

Their voices trailed off, but my daughter had set someone else up to win. Cheering was in *her* blood, too. *Nice job, Whitey!* I wanted to raise my arms in victory and shout my praise loud enough for the entire gym population to hear. But I remembered the long-ago instructions given a B-team cheerleader: stay down and keep quiet. Cheerleading is also an art.

Mom looked like she needed some encouragement. "Hey, Mom? Kati's dance tryouts are next Friday. How 'bout Saturday for an all-day, all-night girl party? I'll bring the treats. You don't have to do a thing."

I was excited to spend undistracted time with her, something I would've been coming up with excuses to avoid a year ago. It was apparent that God was excited too, because the calendar had an unusual blank square only a week away. Winter break was coming, there was a bye on Mom's chemo schedule, and 2003 was almost upon us. Time together would reset our minds and reprioritize busy schedules. Mom had fallen off of mine due to all the running I'd been doing.

She nodded, tight-lipped, arms crossed over her chest. A year ago, I would've assumed she was angry. But I knew what lay beneath that coat was marred beyond recognition. She was playing defense, determined not to let anyone see her weakness or lose heart. I fought back the tears and put on a brave smile like her. We were doing everything we could to make it through to the end of our games.

* * *

Sunday morning came early after a late and perilous drive home from the tournament. We barely made it to church, then barely had time to change out of our church clothes at home before we were due back at the church to prepare for a concert. I'd just dropped into my favorite chair when Chuck walked past me wearing a cowboy hat, carrying a guitar, and doing his Willie Nelson impersonation. "On the road again . . ."

I handed him a deadpan look. I wasn't in the mood. "Think this will go as late as the last concert?"

"I don't know. Why?"

"We were gone all day yesterday. I haven't done any Christmas shopping. The laundry's piled up. I need to go to the grocery store. Oh, and I need to get a lesson plan together for this week's homeschool." I kept forgetting about that last detail, now that I was also in charge of educating our son.

"Stay home, then." He made the decision sound easy.

How could I? I wanted to show my support, but would it have been too much to ask Pastor Tom and Chuck to schedule the concert for after the holidays? I knew the answer. The concert wasn't about me or them. It was planned at the perfect time to cheer on a little guy struggling to find his stage. Of course, I'd go.

"You know I wouldn't miss it."

"Scuze me, Mom." Chapin squeezed past me, carrying a guitar

case as long as he was tall. It bumped along his leg, making it hard to walk.

"Hey, Bud, let me get that." I reached for the handle.

"No, he's got it. Don't ya?" At one touch of Chuck's steady hand, Chapin appeared to grow three inches before striding out to the car.

"Wow." I stared at my husband. I'd forgotten how handsome he was.

"What now?"

"Nothing. I'm just glad I married you." Sometimes, you almost miss the good that's right in front of you. I was surrounded by good.

We entered the church when the sanctuary lights were still dim, creating a sense of calm. It was rare for me to arrive that early. Most Sundays, I raced in breathless after attempting to squeeze one more errand into a claustrophobic week that made breathing and rest impossible. I made a mental note. *Get to church earlier from now on.*

"Check. Check. Check." Chuck's voice boomed through the quiet.

At the back of the church, the doors swooshed open and closed. The church was filling quickly, but Mom and Dad, typically early, were nowhere in sight.

Pastor Tom and Chuck took their places on the stage. Chapin sat waiting in the wings.

"Hey, everyone. Welcome to Community Bible. I'm Pastor Tom, here tonight with my buddy Chuck, and we're gonna play a few songs for you. Thanks for coming. Hope you enjoy the music."

My hands started to sweat, though I wasn't performing. It happened at every concert, maybe because a part of me was up there on that stage. Chuck closed the gap between him and his microphone, casually strumming the guitar.

"Like Tom said, I'm Chuck." He smiled at his pastor friend. "We really appreciate you coming out to hear us tonight. To get us goin', here's a little song I wrote called 'The Bottom's Deep.' Hey, Chapin! How about helpin' us out?"

I applauded wildly as our son walked to the microphone. The kid was a natural like his dad. But my stomach dropped when a glint of uncertainty flashed across his face. The quickest way for a mother to hit rock bottom is to see her child heading in that direction when she could have prevented it.

"He'll be fine! Let him try!" Chuck said as we stood at the top of the steepest slide in the water park years ago. I knew Chapin was too young, but I let myself be convinced that a mother doesn't always know best.

When our son jumped, his cry for help haunted me for years. But I learned a painful lesson that I carried into homeschooling. Mothers can push fear aside and sacrifice themselves for their kids. I went after him. He was worth it.

Seeing Chapin quickly regain his confidence was proof that God hears a mother's prayers, even ones made traveling at the speed of sound.

Where are my parents? They can't miss this! A glance over my shoulder provided a replay view of a past event I'd never witnessed. Mom and Dad stood silhouetted in the doorway, arm in arm. The music began, and they slowly descended the aisle as if in a wedding procession. Mom's well-worn Bible served as a bouquet. Who would stand as her witness when she reached the altar to pledge her life to this man? I would if she asked me. It would have been an honor.

I stepped out into the aisle to let them in, and Kati scooted down as far as she could. For years of Sundays, I'd inhabited these very pews among God's people—in Mom's arms, on her lap, sprawled under or climbing over the seat, sitting still or, like my daughter eventually, squirming with uncontrollable giggles an arm's length out of reach. Three generations now sat in the row, a few short of the 1,000 generations on Mom's secret prayer list. Week after week, she carried me into the presence of God with a weary, wounded soul. She never stopped believing. With God as my witness, I'd do the same.

At the last strum of "The Bottom's Deep," the crowd went wild. I jumped to my feet, clapping furiously, and gave in to temptation. My long, shrill whistle drew some stares. Didn't these people know I had Pentecostal in me?

I tipped over to Mom's side of the pew. "Wasn't he great?"

Her head had remained on Dad's shoulder throughout the applause. She lifted it for a second. "So good," she agreed before laying her head back down.

She must be tired. It's getting late. I glanced back at the clock above the doors. I hoped she could make it to the concert's end.

One after another, the songs kept coming, while Mom and I sat thigh to thigh as we had long before so many misunderstandings came between us. I studied the wooden cross on the wall behind the singers, so grateful that it had hung over our lives all these years. I still didn't understand the pain that accompanied such love, but I had finally identified what was needed to draw closer to the cross. It was the very thing I couldn't put my finger on when I first re-entered these doors. The grace of God had led me back home.

Please, Jesus, let this last, I pleaded. *Let the songs keep playing. Let our lives keep going. Please don't take her away.*

Too soon, familiar chords floated through the air, then the lyrics of the night's last song, "About Good-bye."

> "Momma drops the baby off at day care.
> Daddy picks her up in junior high.
> One day, they'll be driving her to college,

Blinking back the teardrops in their eyes."

Life was short. People were precious. But God is good. The proof was all around me.

> "Tell the ones you love how much you love them.
> Don't take for granted one goodbye . . ."[23]

The song's meaning held every soul captive and lingered in the air along with one final guitar strum. The pews creaked as people reached for their coats and each other. Light flooded the room and broke the spell.

I faced Mom, taking her shoulders in my hands, unwilling to rush, unaware, through another encounter with the angel that guarded my way.

"Thanks for coming, Mom."

I knew better than to expect *You're welcome.* Mom refused to take credit for what God had done. It was because of His goodness and mercy that we stood there in that place together. Goodness and mercy had brought us back together and would follow us all the way Home.

I learned that from her.

Another truth dawned on me as I looked into her dark, glassy eyes and saw my reflection. Neither of us had ever wanted the song to end.

---

[23] "About Good-Bye" by Chuck White and Morgan Cryar.

Chapter 12

Holding Hope

With the busy weekend behind me, I thought I could rest, but I was mistaken. I tossed and turned most of the night, the picture of Mom rubbing her arm during the concert looping through my head on continuous replay. Were the pain pills working? Was she able to get any sleep? The thought of her suffering through the night was torture. I felt her pain in me. "Momma," I mumbled as I fell in and out of the nightmare.

At some point, I succumbed to exhaustion, buried beneath layers of blankets and a patchwork quilt that needed fixing. A shrill ring startled me before dawn.

"Nikki?" Dad's voice bolted me upright. Hadn't I known something was wrong?

"Dad? What's goin' on?"

"We're in the ER. Your mom had some trouble breathing. We went to St. Joe's first, then they sent us here."

"I'm on my way," I said, hanging up before realizing I didn't know where I was going.

Bleary-eyed, I couldn't find my slippers, so I padded to the kitchen barefoot. I stared blankly at the coffee maker, feeling the chill of stone tiles begin to seep in through the soles of my feet.

Chuck's gentle footsteps followed me. "I'll make the coffee. Go shower."

"But you have to leave soon. You'll be late for your plane." The airport was an hour away, and forty-five employees and their families depended on him making his business trip. "Who'll take the kids?" I was fully waking up to the reality of the situation.

"I'll call my mom. You need to go." But so did he. "I can cancel," he said.

I knew he could and would, but I thought he shouldn't. This could be another false alarm. Our marriage had experienced more than its share.

* * *

Pitch black and soundproof, the hotel room promised a good night's rest until the fire alarm rang. A flashing red light on the ceiling announced that there'd be no rest for the weary or the wicked. From reading the hotel guide earlier, I knew guests must calmly proceed to the parking lot. *If you can find it, that is.*

"You've got to be kidding me," Chuck mumbled, trying to put on his pants as I groped through the shapes of clothes in our carry-on, hoping to encounter something decent to wear.

"Wait!" We collided head-on.

"What the—?"

"I need my purse!" It had our credit cards and my lipstick, everything we'd need to rebuild our life after the hotel burned to the ground.

Time was of the essence; the alarm blared louder and faster, urging us to exit quickly and quietly down the stairs, single file. I grabbed hold of the tail of Chuck's T-shirt, letting him lead, but he couldn't find the door. We ricocheted like pinballs, corner to corner, tripping over a wastebasket and shoes. I stayed on his heels like a dog on a bone. We were in this together for better or worse, for richer or poorer, for the rest of our days, which were probably ending that night.

When the all clear was given, we laughed until I cried, thinking how true it was that a good crisis reveals what's most important to you. The first thing you grab is what you think you need to survive.

* * *

I didn't have time to cry or the luxury of riding Chuck's coattails through today's confusion. It was time to go through the fire alone.

After several wrong turns through our neighborhood, I pointed the car in the right direction. Dad had called back, so I knew where to go. The hospital was at the other end of town, giving me time to formulate a plan for the day. I'd check in with Mom and Dad and see what the doctors say. She might have to stay a night or two while they adjusted her meds. If all went well, I'd get them lunch, let them rest while I did some Christmas power shopping at the nearby mall to keep me on track for the holidays.

And if all didn't go well? I pushed that negative thought aside. *Focus on the road. Focus on the good.* This little bump in the journey would be behind us soon. Putting things behind you was the way to move forward, but circumstances were careening out of control.

Remember, God's in control. Mom's words bounced through my head. I hoped one day they'd permanently lodge in my heart.

The road was empty except for a lone car or two, probably some lost soul trying to get home from the bar or an ambitious one heading to work early. I doubted anyone on the road was traveling to my destination. At the railroad crossing, I stopped and looked both ways. Sometimes, people didn't stop; they kept going, thinking they could outrun what was barreling toward them. That's how people died.

I should've stopped and prayed before I turned the key in the ignition. But I could barely think. Who could I call to help me think at this ungodly hour? Mom, Dad, and Chuck weren't available. Josh was on Mountain Standard Time. Who was my next of kin?

"Sande, it's me." For all the times I tried to pin blame on my church past, I found Sande blameless. Somewhere between our eyes first locking across the church campground during a fierce game of Red Rover and the moment I handed her my wedding bouquet to hold, Sande had become family.

It had been a while since we talked, but we never let insignificant details like that get in our way. "Mom's in the hospital. I think she's getting worse. Will you pray? I can't."

Had I ever asked her to pray for me? She and I had observed our mothers at the altar praying for their families' salvation while we sat in the back pew praying that the Dairy Queen wouldn't close before church let out. Prayer ran through our blood. Growing up in church, we didn't receive a faith transfusion, only a continuous drip that was enough to bring us to life.

"Dear Jesus," she said. After that, I heard nothing, but I was sure Jesus did. As she prayed, I pressed the phone to my ear, forcing faith inside. As she called out to God, I stepped on the gas, racing past a blur of buildings. "Amen," she eventually said.

When I looked up, the traffic light was turning yellow. Should I stop or gun it? I slammed on my brakes, my heart pounding. A delivery truck raced past. "Amen. Thank you. I love you; I'll call you later." I hung up and focused on the road.

The sky was tinted pink, meaning a sunrise was ahead. What was it about the morning that filled me with such hope? Maybe that was because I automatically connected mornings to Mom.

She wasn't a morning person; that much was clear. Dad bounced around the house on his toes at the crack of dawn. Mom's slippered steps were more deliberate, as if she wanted to ensure that the floor would hold her before racing headlong into the day.

But no matter what had transpired the day before—slamming kitchen cabinets, clanging pots and pans, a hairbrush swatting at my bottom, or a nightmare requiring her to rush up the stairs to my side—there was always a sunrise the next morning. I'd steal downstairs early, knowing full well that the lamplight in the living room glowed on Mom's open Bible pages in her lap. Whatever lay behind us, hope lay ahead.

"Because of the Lord's great love we are not consumed," she once read aloud to me from Lamentations. "For his compassions never fail," she instructed me to believe. "They are new every morning."[24] Forgiveness was a certainty on the horizon, regardless of the prior day's darkness. I had trouble believing that God's love had no limits. I feared a future morning when I'd wake up, open the door, and find no sunrise. But I never shared that fear with anyone, even Jesus. Didn't He already know?

As I approached the hospital, a wave of nausea hit me. I'd forgotten to eat, and it was too late now. I followed the Emergency signs. The ER doors loomed in the distance. I'd been in this place before.

* * *

Chuck pointed to the words stenciled on the door and raised his brows. "Don't Push. Seriously, now."

I inhaled through my nose and smiled, exhibiting a brave sense of humor. We weren't at the maternity ward yet; there'd be plenty of time for pushing later. "You're gonna' have to work on that delivery," I bantered back.

So far, my entry into motherhood had been easy. Labor had started a couple of hours before, and I'd sailed through each contraction with stellar Lamaze technique. However, I'd been told that the most agonizing hours of my life lie ahead.

---

[24] Lamentations 3:22–23 (NIV).

Chuck and I settled into the birthing center, laid back in recliners, and turned on the TV. If I didn't know better, I'd guess we'd checked into a nice, clean hotel room with an ice machine down the hall.

The "vacation" ended abruptly; I wanted to go home. But first, I needed to give birth to this baby who was not cooperating with my birth plan. I changed attitudes and positions, stripped down to a pair of very unattractive blue hospital socks, and huffed and puffed, nearly blowing my cool. Everyone tried to tell me that some of the most exquisite treasures are found at the end of such agonizing roads, but I refused to listen.

We're better off not knowing what's to come, or we'd never enter the room.

* * *

If I'd known at Kati's birth what I knew now, I would've pushed harder to get her quicker. I would have burst through the hospital doors and let out long, guttural groans until every ounce of my strength was spent. Love was worth it. Knowing Kati was worth the pain.

But I wasn't birthing Mom; I was doing everything possible not to bury her. When the hospital doors swung open, I forced my feet ahead.

"Nikki!" Dad's pale face zigzagged through the waiting room toward me. He wasn't smiling; therefore, it wasn't good. Dad wore a perpetual smile through the worst possible news. "She's in surgery."

I received the information midhug. When I let go, it was as if I wasn't there but in an audience watching someone else's life implode. To cover up my shock, I went through now all-too-familiar motions. "There must be coffee around here. Here's a chair, Dad. Why don't you sit? I'll be right back."

Dad obeyed, looking like the little boy version of him I never knew. Those turquoise eyes had lost sparkle. On the way to the coffee machine, I made a mental note in the family's imaginary war chronicles. *December 9, 2002. We lost our general today.*

After dumping a heap of powdered cream in one cup and pouring the other straight black, I hurried back to find Dad gone. A frantic search located him by the doors to the surgical wing, shaking hands with a tall man in scrubs. Indignant, I marched over.

"Is Mom OK?" It was rude to butt in, but there was little time for niceties. I frowned at the doctor, whose eyes responded with kindness. He spoke softly, describing what was done to help Mom. "It went well. She should be more comfortable after the chest tube drains."

"Chest tube?" I looked from the doctor to Dad, who looked almost guilty. There was something he wasn't telling me. The doctor placed a reassuring hand on my shoulder, then excused himself for another surgery.

"Dad? Do you know what he's talking about?"

"We wanted to tell you in person." Not this again. Could we please have one conversation face-to-face that involved good news?

I let Dad lead me to a little nook with two tan vinyl chairs. He waited for me to sit first, then dropped into the other chair. Where had I left my coffee? I scanned the nearby counters. Did I have time to grab another?

Dad's expression said no. I frowned, reading the lines on his forehead like an obituary. "Your mom and I decided something when we got here. She's stopping the chemo. It's too much."

"So, alternative treatments, then? Mexico?"

"No. I'm sorry. She's tired and can't fight anymore. She hopes you'll understand."

I didn't. I couldn't understand any of this. Where was God

in the middle of this mess? How much time was left? One more Christmas? Easter? Recital? Birthday? We could push through each one together, then do it all again when the next year came. I coached myself like the good Christian girl I strove to be. Mom stopped treatment; she didn't stop living.

A nurse approached. "Family of Lynn Bliss?" Dad and I both jumped up. "She's in recovery now, but she'll be in room 202 after. You can wait there if you like."

"Dad, why don't you go to the cafeteria and get something to eat? It'll probably be a while. I'll wait in her room in case she gets out before you return." At this point, it was all about time and logistics.

I pushed the door open to Mom's assigned room and peeked behind the curtains around both beds. The room was empty, a good sign. This wasn't the kind of room where people stayed and got comfortable. It was the kind of room where people got in, got out, and headed home.

Not willing to waste a minute, I rummaged through my purse for paper and a pen so I could make a list. I wrote "#1" at the top, then I tapped my lips with the pen. Hmmm. *What's the most important thing to accomplish today?* "Everything," I wrote, then I threw the paper and pen back in my purse.

The sound of smooth, clicking wheels approached, and a metal cart hit the wood door, sounding like a gong. Ready or not, here Mom came. I wrestled the urge to run and hide. Besides, there was only one way out; I'd have to crawl right over her and that enormous object riding along on the gurney.

Is that a jug? I pressed back against the wall to give the orderlies room to get by, smiling my best stranger smile since we hadn't been formally introduced. The team of four danced around Mom, pale green figures lifting, pulling, tucking, solemnly nodding while checking off boxes on a paper attached to a clipboard. One by one, they left, until a single nurse remained. Mom acknowledged my presence with a weak smile while the nurse examined the monitors.

"Hi, Mom." I waited to say more. The situation demanded privacy. I pretended to look around, stealing glances at her pale, petite frame swallowed up in a sea of white. The large jug sat atop her torso, gently rocking like a buoy on water as she breathed. Mom's black-and-blue arms clung to it as she was told. I couldn't help but stare. It was an archaic piece of medical equipment. What's next? *Saws and leeches?*

The nurse made one more scribble against the clipboard. "OK, Lynn. Press the button if you need anything." She touched Mom's blanket-covered leg and headed for the door.

"Um, excuse me?" I smiled sweetly, pointing to the elephant in the room. "Are you leaving that?"

The nurse looked clueless.

"The jug? The jar? Are you going to leave it there? On top of her?"

"It's necessary for her comfort."

"Comfort? Are you serious?" I didn't know whether to laugh or cry, so I glared at the nurse, then looked back to Mom, whose eyes pleaded with me to stop. Fine, I'd take charge myself.

I took hold of the jug, then halted. It was attached to her chest by plastic tubing; one end disappeared in the folds of her hospital gown, and the other snaked through the mouth of the jug and dangled there. To highlight the problem further, a trickle of pink ran through the tube and splashed into the bottom of the jar. Mom shook her head ever so slightly, as if to warn me to quit while I was ahead.

My arms dropped to my sides. It was her burden to bear. I couldn't help lift it.

The nurse's expression softened; she must have a mother, too. She adjusted Mom's gown to lessen the tug before she left, a move that honored Mom.

If suffering was inevitable, we must hold on to our dignity. I learned that from her.

Chapter 13

Making Room

The door closed behind the nurse with a click. The lights were bright, the walls stark, the curtain much too thin, and the furnishings sparse. It was Mom, me, and that jug. There was nowhere to hide.

That never stopped me from trying before. When the pain was too much, I'd crawl inside myself if I could. But that wasn't safe either.

* * *

You can't avoid pain, people said. But people said a lot of things, like that the second birth goes much faster. I didn't believe them until I was doubled over in a hospital bed, panting like a crazed animal.

Chuck left to get ice chips and returned to find his overly pregnant wife missing. After a thorough search, he caught sight of my hospital socks peeking out from behind the bed and stuck his face between the metal bars. "What're you doing?" he asked.

I thought it was apparent. "Trying to hide." But the pain found me anyway.

* * *

With the walls closing in, I wanted to bolt. But I couldn't leave her. I wouldn't.

"Momma!" In need of refuge, I gently approached, careful not to disturb the tube and wires snaking around her. I touched my head to her collarbone, not allowing its weight to fully rest on her. That's how it had been since we began, permitting a part of me to touch her, yet afraid to trust her with all of who I was.

I felt her hand struggle to free itself from the sheets and touch my hair. She stroked my head haltingly, a feeble attempt to unsnarl my soul. "There, there," she cooed with a raspy, muffled voice that undid me, until I wept for all the times I couldn't weep in her presence. My treasure chest broke open like Mary Magdalene's, and I poured out all the love I'd been saving, wiping my nose with Mom's gown, then the back of my hand. It was messy, so unlike us, love mixed with pain—a human birth, yet a holy extravagant offering I could no longer hold back.

Machines hummed and whirred; a monitor kept a steady beep, and my eyelids grew heavy. Inches from my face, a trickle of pink liquid ran down into the jar. When would I wake from this nightmare?

"Momma," I whispered, ashamed of my need. I should be holding her.

"You are my smart, beautiful baby girl," she whispered fiercely, reading my shame and piercing through it. I knew that tone. She was the authority, and I wouldn't argue with her. I was done fighting for my independence; I was hers.

I squeezed my eyes shut, tears escaping, winding through our tangled limbs like the tube she bore with such dignity. "You are mine," she added with finality. She was mine; I was hers. The simple words rang true in my heart, like a long-lost lullaby reaching through the dark.

Jesus loves me; this I know, for the Bible tells me so. Two years ago, Mom sang that at the grave of her mother, a woman who wasn't sure she was loved. Why do we know without a doubt that it's true? Because Jesus said so, that's why.

My mind locked on the standard church reply to any inquiries about one's well-being. *God said it, I believe it, and that settles it!* Always, the saying floated through the air in search of those who needed to claim it, barely sticking its landing when the ground gave way under your feet.

And there was more to the story of love. To Jesus, love's not merely a word; it's an action. Jesus said so, then He did so. He laid down His life for me. And Momma did the same in her quiet way.

Laying so close brought us back to our humble beginnings. My birth story was told in fragmented pieces, but I'd often imagined the details.

* * *

"It's a girl!" the doctor announced. He passed me to a nurse, who presented me to a young raven-haired beauty as a gift.

Looking down at me and back at her, the nurse laid me in Mom's arms and connected us with a blessing. "Your daughter looks just like you, Mrs. Bliss."

"Hello, baby," Mom whispered, overcome by an emotion she'd learned to deny up until then. Pressing her lips ever so gently to the softness of my head, she sang an impromptu lullaby. "I love you. You're my smart, beautiful baby girl."

One whimper brought the nurse rushing over with a bottle. Lynn knew the first step would be the hardest if she were going to be the mother she wanted to be. For months, she'd scoured library books, determined to give her baby everything she never had. But no manual on the shelves showed a mother how to bare her soul to her daughter. So she did what she could.

"I'm going to nurse her." Past shame colored her cheeks as she bravely removed one arm from the hospital gown and offered me the very best she had to give.

She gave me everything she knew how to surrender. I had no idea what her surrendering cost her until I became a mother. Even then, part of me had resented every drop.

* * *

I sat up to stretch my arms and legs and stuttered a sigh, fully awake at last. "I love you, Mom." How many times had I said those words without thinking? Never again would I take them for granted. They were etched in my heart.

"I love you, too. I . . . I . . ." There was fear in her eyes.

"Mom, what's wrong?" She sealed her lips, unwilling to tell, determined to bear it alone. "Please tell me." I wasn't asking as a daughter but as a friend. I waited. She looked down at the linoleum, where a white, crinkled wrapper had escaped the janitor's broom. I got up and tossed it in the trash.

Finally, she spoke in a faraway, breathy tone, as if she existed outside her broken body. "The nurses. I heard them. In the operating room, I heard one talk." Then Mom released a pitiful yelp, the sound of a soul being crushed.

"What nurse? What'd she say?" A contact chart hung on the wall. I stood, ready to charge out and locate the perpetrator. Was it Linda? Debbie? Who'd want to hurt this sweet woman?

"I don't know which one said it. It was in the operating room. A nurse asked the doctor why they were putting in a chest tube. She said, 'She's going to' . . . She said, 'She's going to die anyway. Why go to the trouble?' "

"What? No! NO! You are NOT going to die! Why would she say that? She's an idiot! A stupid, frickin' IDIOT!" I wiped fresh tears from my eyes with a determined fist.

But the unidentified nurse had named the real enemy. Death. For months, we'd refused to call the enemy what it was, fearing that we'd somehow brought its approach on ourselves. Now, the cumbersome glass jug slowly, steadily filled, taunting us that we were losing this battle, even though, after all these years, we'd finally won the war.

At once, a hospital gurney exploded through the door. With no formal notice, Mom had a groaning roommate. A gaggle of noisy relatives filed past the foot of Mom's bed, eyeing the jug and nodding their apologies.

While they walked by, I examined my cuticles. Now that all my energy was directed toward Mom, I had no time for new friends. Besides, our family preferred to stay in our own little world.

A curtain was drawn. On the other side, chair legs screeched, dragged across the floor for setting up a card game while the patient rattled off her ailments to the sympathetic crew. I hoped she got better soon, very soon, so we could have our room back. A hand appeared and pulled the threadbare curtain between patients closed a few inches more, seemingly in case *we* might disturb *them*.

The door swung open again, and Dad appeared, with the doctor I'd met earlier. "Mrs. Bliss, how are you feeling?"

Conversation ceased on both sides of the curtain. Mom dipped her head, and more pink liquid ran down the tube.

I'd answer for her. "She's doing great, Doctor. She'll be out of here soon, right? She's a fighter." I was a fighter, too. I liked being on her side. "When can she go home?"

"Hmm." He hesitated, hugging his clipboard to his chest. "We'll see." With his narrowed eyes, was he assessing my ability to attack? "It wouldn't be prudent to move her right now. More fluid needs to drain. But we'll see, OK?" He smiled at Mom and patted her arm. "Mrs. Bliss, do you have any questions?"

She shook her head and closed her eyes, dismissing him. I bit my tongue, though I wanted to track down and report that nasty nurse. The doctor bowed slightly and turned to go.

"Dr. J?" I hoped the doctor didn't mind my calling him by the abbreviation I'd heard my parents use. My mom's life was in his hands.

"Yes?" His thick lenses magnified dark brown eyes in which I saw a compassionate man, one who bore the impossible weight of telling the truth and keeping the faith. I pressed my lips together. I couldn't lay another burden on him, couldn't force him to promise me anything more than to do his best.

How many times in a day did he hear the question *Am I going to die?* What was his usual answer? It was a question I'd prefer to kick down the road.

As challenging to answer was a question I'd not considered in thirty-eight years. *Am I going to really live?* Like Mom, I didn't want to know life's brevity, so I shook my head and let the doctor walk out the door.

"I'll be back," I said to Dad.

Dr. J had turned right, presumably to make his rounds. I turned left, on another mission.

"Excuse me?" I leaned across the nearest counter, which looked to be a place where important people made decisions. Red-and-green tinsel garland draped the work area, and "Jingle Bells" floated up from a hidden radio underneath. It must be hard to keep the Christmas spirit in a place where no one wants to be.

The busy hospital clerk looked up, brows raised, pen poised on a stack of forms. Her composure was impressive; I'd also been a pen pusher, in a job where every person that appeared was another obstacle to getting work done.

"Who do I talk to in order to get my mother a private room?" I'd made similar requests while traveling. *Do you have a room with a view? Maybe by the pool?* But this was no luxury vacation. We required sanctuary.

"Um. Can I get back to you later today?"

"Thanks, but this is an emergency." Eyes pleading, I held my ground.

Refusing to look at me, she threw down the pen, picked up the phone and dialed a number, then swiveled her chair to have a low conversation with someone on the other line. She's a person, I reminded myself. *She's probably someone with kids at home, Christmas presents to be bought, and dinner to cook. The holidays are stressful enough as they are.*

Nervous, I looked around. Patients on gurneys lined the hallway, waiting to be seen or to recover in the next available bed. *Dear Jesus, please give Mom a room.* It was a frivolous request; she already had a room, and many others didn't. But this was Mom; privacy was essential to her comfort, and I knew she'd rather suffer in silence than ask for what she felt she didn't deserve. Ask and you will receive, right?[25] I wasn't asking for me; I was asking for Mom. She deserved the best.

The clerk spun back around and covered the phone receiver with her hand. "I think a private room has become available on the next floor."

Stunned, I nodded.

"I'm not sure insurance will cover—"

"I'll pay the difference."

"OK then. I'll send the orderlies to move her when the room's ready."

"Thank you!" I wanted to jump over the counter and hug her. "Thank you. You have no idea . . ." Her face softened with a sad smile. Maybe she did.

Back in Mom's room, a full-blown party was in progress on the other side of the curtain. I sat down, barely able to contain the

---

[25] Matthew 7:7 (CEV).

news of the private room. But with the noise coming from behind the curtain, it was hard to get a word in edgewise.

Mom, Dad, and I raised our brows and shook our heads, our attention ricocheting between the curtain and each other. Our little movements were family code boiling down to an exercise in decorum. *I cannot believe how rude those people are*, Mom and Dad were signing. *But we are Christians, so we will not comment on how disrespectful they are. Instead, we will endure and dislike them in silence.*

"RUDE!"

There, I'd said it. It couldn't be helped. Sitting with my parents, I'd reverted to my teenage self.

The noise behind the curtain paused. Then the visitors there turned up the volume.

"Nicole!"

"Sorry, Mom. But hey, I've got some news. I found a private room." As if on cue, the orderlies arrived. "Whoa. Now that's service."

I gathered Mom's few belongings, but the quick change unsettled me. Why was everyone so anxious to keep Mom here?

"We're moving to another room," I called over my shoulder, as if the strangers cared. "Good-bye!" And good riddance, I thought, then I thought again. This wasn't how I wanted to leave a room, even a rude one. When I leaned back through the doorway, a visitor with a curious face leaned back in a chair. "I hope you all get to go home soon," I said. "Merry Christmas."

We squeezed into the elevator with more strangers. Mom was flat on her back, pinned down by the jug. The rest of us lined the walls. After the doors closed, I noticed we weren't moving. Then we moved too slowly. My mind said the strangers were taking up all the air. I was going to die. *Inhale, exhale.* My palms were cold and sweaty; my neck was hot.

Mom reached out. "Honey, are you OK?" Even a month ago,

her pity would have annoyed me. Now, it humbled me. She was afraid she was dying, but she was worried about me.

Two chimes later, the doors opened, and fresh air swooshed in. The hall was vacant except for a petite, smiling nurse waiting to show us to our room. "I'm Cara. Please let me know if you need anything, absolutely anything." She pointed at her desk as we walked by.

If it weren't for the fluorescent bulbs and smell of rubbing alcohol, we could've been on our way to a hotel room, breathlessly anticipating what we'd find when we opened the door. Would it be a room with a view or one that overlooked the air-conditioning unit? In my experience, the view always determined the success of the trip.

Chuck also had a theory, in which the view from your room exposed what the hotel clerk thought of you. He thought she peered over her reading glasses and asked herself, *Am I going to surprise them with something wonderful or give them what I think they really deserve?* Could I have been nicer to the hospital clerk? I guess I'd find out soon.

In some ways, I regarded God's thoughts as like those of Chuck's hotel clerk. *Do you want the best? Then you better be on your best behavior, missy.* It didn't matter how much you paid; more would be required.

Buried in the pages of Mom's Bible was another story. "I go to prepare a place for you," Jesus said.[26] If Jesus was preparing it, it had to be perfect, a place without tears, cancer, pain, or broken hearts.

One day, Mom would enter a heavenly room already made ready. The walls were rolled with buttermilk-yellow paint, the color of her beloved sewing room. In the room's center, a four-poster

---

[26] John 14:2 (KJV).

with a feather mattress was piled a mile high with faded patchwork quilts. A nearby window overlooked a meadow. After a delightful visit with her mother next door, Mom would gather flowers to put in a vase of milk glass, maybe a sprig of Baby's Breath to tickle her nose and remind her of me. One day, Mom would rest in a perfect place.

One day.

So before I pulled back the curtains in her new hospital room, I made a decision. Whatever view someone gave us would be the view God meant for us to have in the present, and I'd be grateful.

I'd learned that from her.

Chapter 14

No Regrets

"Hmmm. Well, at least I can keep an eye on my car." I grinned before turning from the view of the parking lot. Seeing Mom in a private room was a sight to behold, better than any window view I'd expected.

"Can I get you guys anything?" I checked my watch. "I'm gonna check on the kids. It's gettin' late; I'm not sure anyone gets discharged after dinnertime."

Wandering down the corridor, I held my flip phone to every outside wall to find a cell signal until I happened to run into Cara, who loaned me the desk phone. "Anytime!" she replied when I thanked her, but I hoped I didn't have to ask again other than to line up Mom's homecoming party.

"Hello?" Hearing my daughter's voice made me instantly homesick. It was one thing to be away from my kids for a planned weekend trip, quite another not to have an itinerary in my purse.

"Hey, honey. How was school?" I waited, anticipating what Kati's response would be.

"Is Nanny OK? When are you coming home?" She was fifteen but still my little girl—Nanny's girl, too.

"She's doin' pretty good. The doctors are helping her get better." My voice rose half an octave with the lie. "I'm gonna' stay with her tonight. Hopefully, we'll get out of here bright and early tomorrow, OK?" I needed Kati to be OK. If she wasn't, then I couldn't be anywhere but with her.

Next in the phone line was her brother. "Grandma Barb got me a new game!" God bless my mother-in-law, who'd stepped in at a moment's notice without hesitation. Whenever she showed up, it was with shopping bags and Tupperware containers of love. "I love you, bud. Can I talk to Grandma?"

"Nikki?" Barb's voice dropped. "How's Lynn?"

"OK. Well, not really. I can't talk about it. I'm sorry. Looks like Mom's here for the night. Would you mind staying there?" I knew the answer. Chuck's Mom was a saint and a walking miracle.

Barb had seen more than her share of hospital rooms, almost dying herself at the young age of forty-four. By an act of God, she'd been inches away from the best heart surgeons in the world when she was moments away from death. Barb was living proof that good prevailed. I hung up, believing that it would.

After making very unhealthy selections at the vending machine, I returned with my arms full of enough junk food to keep us all busy. It might be a long night.

The hallway was empty, the door to Mom's room ajar. It was quiet. Maybe they were both sleeping. Exhausted myself and unable to imagine how they felt, I tiptoed to the door before I realized I'd nearly intruded on a tender moment between husband and wife. A better daughter would have discreetly looked away, but I snooped, spellbound by the love scene.

Mom and Dad were affectionate in their children's presence, but I'd never witnessed such intimacy of their souls. Dad held Mom's hands in his, the jar perched precariously on the edge of the mattress between them. I wasn't close enough to interpret their deep conversation, but I understood the desperation.

Their eyes were intent on each other's; their voices rose, fell, and broke like a tragic movie soundtrack. It was a love story I took for granted, one none of us ever assumed would end this way.

Mom spoke, her face upturned to his. Unflinching, she waited for his response. Dad wiped a tear with a hand that wouldn't let go of hers. He nodded and bent close to her with great effort, his lips poised over hers. The sound of one quick kiss vibrated through my chest.

Step away, I thought. *This is private*. But I was paralyzed with grief.

There was another rush of conversation. Mom spoke and waited. Dad wiped another tear off his whiskers and nodded, then stole another kiss.

I forced myself to bear witness, to remember the treasure I'd been given, parents who loved each other until the end. One day, if I ever questioned my own marital commitment, I might have to draw from this scene of raw, unyielding devotion. Two more quick kisses followed, then a lingering one as if it would be the last time their lips ever touched. I couldn't take it anymore.

"I'm back!" I announced, dropping the snacks next to Dad. I kept moving, straightening the tray, organizing the counter, rearranging the chairs, reviewing the chart on the wall—anything to stop thinking about what I'd seen. Mom and Dad's jaws were set, their thoughts lost in another, distant realm.

I had to pull them back. But how? An untouched orange juice caught my eye.

"Remember when Kati passed out in the White House?" There was nothing like grandkids to make a grandparent smile. "The White House doctor ordered her a cookie and an orange juice." Two sets of eyes focused on me, confirming Mom and Dad were hooked.

They hadn't been there that day, and I hadn't been close enough to Kati either. I was waiting outside after the White House tour when her friend burst out of doors marked Do Not Enter and told me that my whole world had collapsed on the other side. The Secret Service agents should've known that a mother would storm the gates of Hell or breach national security to get to her child. Love takes a bullet without thinking. Thankfully, I didn't have to go that far.

Mom and Dad's faces brightened as they pictured the rescue attempt. "You're a good mom, honey," Mom said.

I wasn't good at taking compliments, but I wouldn't refuse this one. "I learned from the best." For once, Mom didn't protest either.

Oblivious to the family history being made before his eyes, Dad had another epiphany. "You know, when you were at the White House, you weren't too far from where I met your mom."

"Oh yeah?" I played dumb. Though I knew the story, I begged to hear it again. It felt good to remember some things are just meant to be.

Though it was difficult to imagine dainty Mom in combat boots, she had a pair when she met Dad in 1962. She was a private in the U.S. Women's Army Corp, and he was also stationed in Washington. They were two soldiers in a city of thousands, so divine intervention must have placed them in the same little dive bar.

Mom was painfully shy, sipping Coca-Cola in a back corner booth out of the line of flirtatious fire. Dad made a beeline to her friend sitting next to her, who had caught his eye. Then something changed the trajectory of history and sealed my future existence.

"Your mom began to laugh! I'd never heard anything like it in my life." Dad chuckled, reminiscing.

Neither of them could recall what had delighted her, but the sound would forever ring in Dad's ears. Her laughter was otherworldly, eternal, a melody of sweet, rushing water that flooded his soul with joy and rose above the din. That laughter drew him to her hazel eyes, then it was game over. Mom had won Dad's heart.

There was some dispute about who made the next move. "Your mom winked at me and convinced me to ask her out."

"Warren, I did no such thing!"

Without fail, love stories have two sides.

* * *

"Your mom asked me to marry her," Chuck informed the kids at the family table.

"I did NOT! What I said was 'Are you ever going to ask me to marry you?' "

"What's the difference?"

"Mom, how old were you?" Kati went straight to the good stuff.

"Um, well, I can't remember," I deflected. "But I know we met at a gathering at your dad's apartment on Christmas night. He was playing guitar and singing to his girlfriend."

"Who I dumped that night. I was trying to break up with her."

"Well, I didn't know that then, but I remember what I thought. *Someday, I want someone to love me like that.* And here we are. Better yet, here you two are!" I grabbed Kati's hand, then Chapin's.

"Ew, Mom! Gross!" Boys aren't fond of love stories.

But girls want to know more. "Why were you at Dad's apartment on Christmas night?"

"Well, that's a long story, but Aunt Sande took me there."

The kids already knew how I met Sande, a story equally unbelievable. Hoping to win a championship game of Red Rover at church camp, she zeroed in on my prissy shirt with a red rose pattern and ruffled sleeves, guessing I was an easy target. Her hunch was confirmed after she and a teammate clotheslined me.

I flew backward and landed in a humiliated heap, hoping to never run into her again as long as I lived. But God had other ideas. Though Sande and I attended different churches miles apart, we ended up in the same Sunday School room months later when Mom decided it was time to go "church shopping."

I sat in the front row while Sande bullied me by yanking on my dress ties from behind. Later in the girls' bathroom, she recognized our camp connection and invited me to be her sidekick for the rest of our lives, a request I was afraid to deny. As time went on I discovered that not only do opposites attract, but they become the best part of you. Sande and I spent weekends, summers, and every possible holiday together, eventually leading to that historic Christmas night.

* * *

My mind boggled at trying to connect the myriad pieces of a puzzle that had to be perfectly aligned to make up an unimaginable picture. Not one to doubt something was part of God's grand plan, I drew comfort from knowing that someone greater was connecting the events of our lives to write one epic story. People can't make up such complicated stuff.

Months after Mom and Dad met at the bar, they married in a hastily pulled-together but elegant affair. Mom suited up in ivory wool; Dad borrowed a suit coat and tie. Two young lovers loaded in a car with a few friends and said their vows in a little chapel for the deaf, the only available church at the time. God must have heard the prayers of their hearts the day they became one with their faces set on the future, backs turned on their pasts.

As a teen, I pressed Mom for more details of her life before Dad, eager to know more about her story. When I did, Mom's eyes fogged, and she frowned at memories she wouldn't share. I mistook her furrowed brow for concentration and kept pressing. "How'd you get to Washington, DC? I thought you lived in Chicago."

"I went on a bus," she said as she walked out of the room. Filing the information in a mental folder labeled *The Mysteries of Mom*, I concluded some puzzles had missing pieces that could never be found.

I did piece together that I was a miracle. Because of Mom's laughter, I came to be. Her ability to laugh through her pain was the greatest miracle of all.

* * *

"Warren, you look tired," Mom said. "Why don't you go get something to eat?"

"Lynn, I'm not leaving you." He wouldn't, so I ganged up on him with Mom.

"Hey, Dad, the cafeteria's open late. Take a break. I'll take good care of her."

"Warren, go!"

"Dad, go!"

"OK, I'll be right back." He shuffled out.

Mom wasted no time, reaching for my hand.

"Need something, Mom?"

"No regrets," she said. She spoke with a mother's authority, commanding my undivided attention.

"Wh—?"

"No regrets," she repeated.

She and I were so different, yet we shared a common trait that kept us from moving forward. I often mocked the madness of woulda, coulda, shoulda—the constant replay of options and indecision that choked the joy out of the most minor choice.

"What would you like, ma'am?" a waitress would ask.

"A burger," I'd say, satisfied until a salad passed by the table. "I shoulda ordered a salad! I've gained five pounds on this vacation."

"I love your new couch!" I once told Mom.

"Really? I woulda ordered blue instead of green if I'd known it clashed so with the fireplace."

Chuck often reassured me at the dining table. "The roast is delicious, Nikki."

"Uh, thanks. I coulda left it in another hour."

The second-guessing was rooted in fear that everything important hinged on our choices; ultimately, we were the ones in control. If we didn't get a decision right, the consequences were irreversible. Bearing the boulders of woulda, coulda, and shoulda on my chest made breathing impossible.

Involuntarily, my gaze went to the contents of the jar on Mom's chest, slowly but steadily rising and falling. It represented a fear neither Mom nor I had any more time to address. But how do you conquer a fear you can't control?

* * *

"Honey, did you pack your suit?" Dad asked Mom.

I held my breath in the back seat. We'd been driving for an hour. If Mom forgot her bathing suit, our annual day trip to Lake Huron wouldn't be the same. Mom barely nodded and looked away.

"Huh?"

"Yes, Warren," she snipped. "I did."

My forehead resting against the window, I watched cornfields whiz by, hoping Mom would be happy when we arrived. A picnic at the park wouldn't be fun if she was angry.

Her mood lifted when water appeared in the distance. "Oh, Warren! Doesn't it take your breath away?" She rolled down the window to let in the summer breeze. I inhaled the aquatic scent that filled the car.

After a picnic of sandwiches and Kool-Aid, Mom disappeared into a rustic changing room and reappeared in a short terrycloth robe, her bathing suit hidden underneath. She ignored Dad's wolf whistle, pulling the robe's hem down and tucking her hair into her swim cap as she approached the water. Facing a green sea that danced and stretched before her, she grabbed the ties of the robe as if trying to decide whether to loosen them or pull them tighter.

I sat on a blanket nearby, toes buried in sand, both afraid Mom would dive in and longing for her to. When Mom swam, she moved through the water with a power she didn't have on the shore, a power I wanted to possess. The woman who sidestepped every mud puddle found the courage to swim into choppy waters.

Somewhere back in time, someone must have taught her how to be fearless in deep water. Did her mother? A snapshot of Grandma crawling on her knees to look out the window of an observation tower had told me that wasn't likely. But I hoped Mom would teach me, one day.

In an instant, she shed her robe and plunged in. Her head popped up in the distance. Dad whooped, waved his arms, and cupped his hands to keep the wind from stealing his words. "Do the butterfly!"

I jumped up and waved my arms, too. "Do the butterfly!" We both wanted Mom to soar.

She rose up and down through the waves, in and out of the water, her arms propelling her through the fresh spray. Mom swam closer and stood, beckoning me to join her. "Want to come swimming with me, Nikki?"

"No!" I stomped to the blanket and rolled into a ball, hiding my face. *Please, come tickle me, carry me into the water, and show me how to be brave.* I wanted her help, but I was too afraid to reach for her hand.

Mom didn't hear the cry of my heart over the water's roar. When I looked up, she was already on the beach, picking her robe off the sand and heading back to change into dry clothes.

Stubbornly clinging to fear, I'd forfeited my chance to fly.

* * *

I never learned to do the butterfly stroke or swim in any polished fashion at all. While I waited for time to make me brave, I slowly lost my nerve. I'd been too proud to ask a woman who navigated the waves to share her secret. Regret over that choice blew in with the scent of any nearby water, a regret I faced daily now that I lived on a lake.

Mom read my face and tightened her grip on my hand. She wasn't going to let me drown on her watch. The waves of regret were bigger than us, but someone greater, more powerful, had taught her how to rise above them. I was finally ready to learn, if she was willing to teach me.

"OK, Mom. No regrets."

There was no reason to fear the wind, the waves, the past, even the future. Love would carry us to the places we were destined to go.

I learned that from her.

Chapter 15

Enjoy Your Life

I woke up to low conversation outside Mom's door. Good. Doctors were making their morning rounds. Maybe Mom could get the OK to go home and get some rest. In case we might've forgotten no one gets any real sleep in hospital rooms, even private ones, we'd had frequent reminders.

At 1:00 a.m., "Lynn, darlin', I'm sorry to wake you, but I need to check your heart."

Again at 2:00 a.m., "Hi, Mrs. Bliss. The doctor asked me to listen to your lungs. How're you feeling?"

And yet again at 3:30 a.m., when slumber was sweetest, "I'm going to mark on the jar so we can keep track of your progress, OK?"

Dad and I had kept one eye open between us all night, each stealing a few minutes of fitful sleep before an unwanted but well-meaning visit from hospital staff. I reminded my sleep-deprived self that everyone had the same goal: getting Mom better to go home.

Dr. J entered with two other doctors he introduced. "Mrs. Bliss, I've asked my colleagues to join me this morning to help us determine the best course of action now."

"Sorry, what do you mean by 'now'?" I interrupted. "Has something changed? We were hoping to get her home today."

The doctors glanced at one another, then Dr. J stepped away from Mom's bed, motioning for Dad and me to follow. He lowered his voice, choosing his words carefully. "Lynn's vital signs are indicating a rapid buildup of fluid around the heart."

"But the jug?" I asked.

"The surgery provided some relief, but the fluid's building faster than we can drain it. I'll consult with my colleagues after their exam, but I believe it would be dangerous to move your mom."

"For now?"

"Yes," Dr. J said, his eyes attempting to say more. I begged them not to.

After a quick nod to each doctor as their troop filed out the door with grim faces, I smiled and gave a quick clap. "OK! Well, I need coffee and a trip to the gift shop for deodorant. Might make a few phone calls. Mom? Dad? Need anything?" Before they could answer, I strolled out, walked a few steps, then half-walked and half-ran, but I couldn't move faster than the tears running down my face.

Cara was on desk duty and pointed at the phone. "Make as many calls as you need to." I tried to smile at her before I started.

"Chuck?" I couldn't say anymore. I didn't have to.

"I'm getting on the next plane. I shouldn't have come to Denver."

"What about your meeting?"

"Screw the meeting. Someone else can handle it. I'm coming home. Have you called your brother?"

"Not yet." I pulled a piece of paper from my wallet and stared at the words underlined at the top—*Emergency Contacts*. Josh and Holly were flying out of the Denver airport in two weeks to spend Christmas with Mom and Dad. Should they wait to come until then? Mom's words popped into my head. *No regrets.* I made the emergency call and then hovered a finger over the next number on the short list.

"Hello?" Thankfully, my mother-in-law picked up on the first ring. I couldn't talk to my kids without losing it.

"Mom's worse than we thought. Please don't say anything to the kids yet. Chuck's on his way home."

When I got to the last number, I realized it should've been my first call. *Isn't that typical?* I'd do all I could to solve a problem before asking for anyone's help, even God's. I dialed the church prayer line and asked for a miracle.

A quick trip to the cafeteria and the gift shop rounded out my errands for the day. I was wired with caffeine and a new resolve to have more faith. It was time for a triumphant return.

"Shower to Shower!" I held up the purple plastic container to show my roommates, who looked puzzled by my great mood. "The clerk said they were all out, but I prayed and found this behind the Reese's Peanut Butter Cups!"

"That's good, honey," Mom said in a raspy voice, not seeming to connect the dots like I had. If God cared enough to hide talcum powder in the candy aisle, why would He stop there? I kept my thoughts to myself; Mom was tired.

Suddenly, the door swung wide open. Dad gave a garbled cry. Mom's brows shot up in surprise. "Shirli! Don? What are you—?"

"Nothing could keep us away." Best friends knew the rules but also when to break them. Sande's parents took turns bending down to delicately wrap their arms around Mom and the octopus-armed medical apparatus tethered to her. Mom's face glowed in their shadow. They walked over to squeeze Dad's shoulders, no doubt making sure he was all there. The Major, as we fondly called Don, faced Dad, took one step back, and stood at attention. But rather than salute his friend, he reached out and shook Dad's hand.

Just like their daughters, Shirli and Mom appeared to be unlikely companions. Shirli liked to color outside the lines by embracing God's grace above a list of church rules. On the contrary, Mom was a list follower. Thrown together when Sande and I became friends, they'd remained close even when life pulled their girls in different directions.

Sande's dad was a man of few words, with a gruff faith no one dared question. Throughout my endless summer weeks spent under his roof, Don had proved to be a bigger-than-life teddy bear.

"Hey, Bliss," he teased tenderly. For some reason, he'd been the one person to see through my false bravado. "Is it still snowing down south?" His whole face broke into a grin, reflecting warmth into steel-blue eyes. It was an ancient joke, but I still knew my lines.

"Nope! No snow today. I've got jeans on. See?" I lifted my knee to demonstrate I didn't have a white slip hanging below a dress hem like in my Sunday School days.

I hugged Shirli, avoiding her sad, gray eyes. I'd always found truth there and couldn't bear to see it now. She rubbed my back as if polishing up all the treasures she used to share with me at her kitchen table. How often had she laid an open Bible beside a plate of Keebler cookies? More than once, she'd pointed me in the right direction, holding her hand up toward Heaven. "You know," she'd say, "there's streets of gold up there." Because of her love for me and Jesus, I constantly came back for more.

Where two or three are gathered in My name . . .[27] That was one of Mom and Shirli's favorite verses. It's claim that Jesus was in our midst had once made me claustrophobic. Now I knew God designed His people to travel in packs, not alone. But no one in this pack of friends had ever gone where we were all eventually headed. Don and Shirli took their seats and settled in for Mom's journey.

---

[27] Matthew 18:20 (NKJV).

With her friends present, Mom took on another persona, confident and funny. "Don, you look tired," she commented, concerned. "Would you like to take my bed for a nap?"

When the shock at her suggestion wore off, we laughed so loudly that a nurse popped in her head to check on the patient. Dad found that even funnier and began to slap his knee, which tickled Shirli's funny bone until she spilled the coffee she'd brought with her onto Don, whose shoulders showed signs of a rumbling snicker. Then a loud sneeze erupted from Don, adding to the comedy show.

Mom's eyes were bright with joy. "Gazoom-tight!" she offered. As the ridiculous word echoed off the sterile walls, I began to giggle uncontrollably.

Eventually, the residual chuckles subsided, and we each stared at a linoleum square in front of us. Private thoughts turning over in our minds while we sipped tepid coffee, we took turns sneaking peeks at Mom, who had closed her eyes.

A sweet alto note from Shirli's lips tiptoed into the silence and led into "Great Is Thy Faithfulness,"[28] a well-worn hymn hummed as a sacrifice of praise, for God's people are given a song in the face of fear. As a young teen, I'd read stories of faithful who'd gone before me, herded into colosseums before lions were released. Faith's voice rose bravely from people huddled around their children and convinced what they were about to suffer wouldn't compare with the streets of gold that awaited.

I was afraid to believe so much, fearing I'd lose everything if push came to shove and faith faltered. But as I joined the singing, fear fell away. Perfect love was present, even as death tried to barricade the door. The song spoke rock-solid truth to support my faith. Nothing could separate us from God and His love.

---

[28] "Great is Thy Faithfulness", by W.M. Runyon (1923).

After returning to church as a mom, I'd had trouble hitting the notes during worship. More than anything, I wanted to sing praise to the God of second chances, but the sounds caught in my throat. Embarrassed, I'd resorted to lip-syncing. Now, my voice returned—not only with power, but with beauty. It sounded angelic, a gift from God.

Let the lions roar, let the chains wrap around the prison bars, let our souls stretch beyond their limits and our hearts break until they bleed. We will sing for His glory in our darkest hour, because He is with us.

Shirli picked up Mom's Bible and began to read. "And I am convinced that nothing can ever separate us from God's love. Neither death nor life, neither angels nor demons, neither our fears for today nor our worries about tomorrow—not even—"

"—the powers of hell," Shirli and I continued in unison. Though my recitation was rusty, it came easier as my memory revived. By the end, I was sure of the words. "Nothing in all creation will ever be able to separate us from the love of God that is revealed in Christ Jesus our Lord."[29]

Shirli closed the Bible with a soft thump and began another song. "Some glad morning when this life is o'er, I'll fly away."[30] Joining her one by one, we comprised a ragtag version of an angelic choir, but my ears have never heard a sound quite like it on earth. Don's vibrato shook our courage loose from any remaining tendrils of fear, and we each stood tall on the inside, our chins and hearts lifted, our hearts and minds without doubt that Jesus walked among us, even now.

Faith didn't surrender to death; it defied it. When Jesus stood at the entrance of Jerusalem and faced His cross, He lifted His chin and set it like flint. Locking eyes with Mom from across the room, I saw a spark in her darkened pupils and knew she saw it in

---

[29] Romans 8:38–39 (NLT).
[30] "I'll Fly Away" by A.E. Brumley, 1929 (Hartford Music Publishing 1932).

me. She tilted her chin ever so slightly, and I followed suit—like mother, like daughter, and, one glorious day, like Christ.

Nothing could stand between Jesus, Mom, and me. I learned that from her.

After losing count of the hours, I noticed the coffee cups were empty. When I offered to get more, Shirli and Don looked at one another. Don slapped his knees and pushed off to stand with a groan, then pulled his wife to her feet.

They hugged Dad, then walked to Mom's bedside to say their goodbyes. Don and Shirli had done all they could. They'd prepared us a table in the presence of our enemy, laid out a picnic blanket on the battlefield, and lent us their strength to press on to the prize.

I shrunk back to let old friends have their final conversation. Shirli bent over and whispered in Mom's ear. "Lynn, my dear, dear sister, what can I do for you? Name it, it's done."

Mom whispered an answer unintelligible from where I stood. Shirli stared into her eyes with understanding, touched her cheek, and nodded. Don and Shirli walked out the door without looking back.

One Mother's Day many years in the future, Shirli would slip me a note that revealed Mom's request. Shirli had no way of knowing that moments before she handed me the envelope, I'd considered shrinking back from my faith and running for the door. God had kept her and Mom's secret safe until I needed to know.

That day in the hospital, Mom needed a miracle more than ever before, but her last prayer request was for me. I unfolded Shirli's stationery and managed to read from it through my tears. Mom's last request? "Please look over my girl."

Dad excused himself from the hospital room to walk our friends to the elevator and stretch his legs. Mom and I sat in silence, the beep of the monitors fading into the background. I sipped on a flat Diet Coke and munched on the last few pretzels in a bag, the snacks reminding me that the long-awaited sleepover scheduled for the following weekend wasn't going to happen. Why hadn't I made the time when I could have?

I felt Mom's eyes on me and knew she was taking inventory. Her gaze traveled to the top of my head; out of habit, I lifted my hand to smooth the frizz. I wouldn't apologize for my appearance; I didn't want her to feel she had to do the same.

Her eyes narrowed, as if she were considering the right words for her strong-willed, bullheaded daughter. She knew better than anyone how skittish I was—how one critique, however kind, would have me bolting out the door. It was painful to be scrutinized after a night and day spent in a chair.

Sorry this is all you got, Mom, I wanted to say. *I wish I were more.*

Her cool hand reached out and rested on mine. I pulled my eyes away from the thick needle piercing her hand's tissue-thin skin. She'd threaded many needles in her day, squinting to find entry to the impossible.

How many Saturday afternoons had Mom taken that same hand and smoothed a new piece of gingham, preparing to pin a pattern on me that I resented? All I wanted was to run out the screen door and into the sunshine, yet she held me captive to make something lovely that I couldn't envision at the time.

It occurred to me that's the way of mothers and daughters. Every fitting takes too long and holds the possibility of all your best efforts being ripped out by the seams when the results are disappointing. Love's work is messy, with uneven stitches and fallen hems, but it's love that binds us together in the end. Grasping Mom's weakened hand, I decided I'd now prefer gingham over any other fabric as long as I lived.

Mom cleared her throat to usher in what she'd been waiting to say. "Enjoy your life."

"What? I do!" The command offended me as if she'd been

biting it on her tongue for years. Did she agree with Chuck and think I was "the warden"? Barking at my kids, stomping around the kitchen, squeezing every drop of water out of discarded washcloths like the joy that often went down my drain? Did she expect me to do better? I was doing the best I could.

And what about her? Had she really enjoyed her life? Hardly so, in my estimation. Who was she to counsel me?

"Enjoy your life." Her repeat of the three simple words confounded me further. Was she somehow regretting her own life? That she needed to say it a second time felt heavy. Once was like saying *Have a nice day.* Twice was to express a forever goodbye.

"Mama?" What was she thinking? How could I enjoy my life without her in it?

Her jaw was set. This wasn't a suggestion. It was a command. I'd waited for such anointing, for her to kiss me on the top of my head and tell me whatever I did was going to be alright.

Don't sweat the small stuff, I'd wanted to hear her say. *Throw your arms up to the sky and run as fast as you can. Don't worry about the rocks and ruts along the way. Run hard! Have fun! Do what brings you joy.* At one time, I would've sold my birthright for this blessing, but not now.

I'd never meant to waste life, but I couldn't quite take hold of life to the full. There was little time for joy. My life was full of laundry baskets, pickup times, grocery lists, flower beds to weed. Most days, motherhood felt like a chore, not a joy.

I had no idea how to change things. But that was what Mom wanted, so I agreed.

"OK, Momma. I will." Maybe joy would come later in life, when my schedule slowed down. Would I be free to watch *Full House* reruns, play in the sandbox, let the housework go? What did she know that I didn't? Could I ever know? This was hardly the time for a two-part lesson.

In our usual mother-daughter fashion, we struggled to

understand that we wanted the best for each other. She wanted me to live my life. I wanted her to keep living.

In that ten-by-ten-foot hospital room, absent of all color, I had no idea how many vibrant blooms would flourish from the tiny seed that Jesus and Mom planted in me that day.

Chapter 16

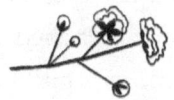

Hope of Glory

"Hey, maybe I could get a job as a hospital tour guide?" Dad's humor made a stab in the dark. We both looked at Mom's lips to see if it hit the target.

Eyes closed, she offered a quick smile, focused on fighting the growing anxiety as her second day in the room was ending. Dad and I could explore the hallways to blow off steam; she could only wander where her thoughts took her.

"Yeah, Dad! Maybe map out a chicken soup for dinner?" Another smile flashed across Mom's face. She and I enjoyed the same dry humor. We also read each other's minds.

"Is your Christmas shopping done?" she asked.

"Not yet. It'll get done. I'm not worried. You?" Why did I say that? *You're an idiot, Nikki!*

She shook her head.

"I'll do yours for you. What're ya thinkin' for the kids?" Neither of us mentioned the possibility that she wouldn't be home to see her gifts opened.

"Bibles."

"Oh?" How many Bibles does a growing boy or girl need? Like

155

me, they had Bibles in all shapes, sizes, and versions lying around, rarely opened. Access to the Book itself wasn't holding up their study. The issue was with their assigned teacher.

* * *

As often as I had rolled my eyes behind Mom's back as she bent over her Bible, I was now hunched over mine. The words I'd memorized in a dutiful drone as a girl jumped off the tissue-thin pages as an adult. I couldn't explain it, but I had to try.

"How was Bible study?" Chuck asked to be polite.

"So good! You can't believe what God showed me! Wait, let me find it." I'd run my finger back and forth over the yellow and pink highlights to locate the exact Word that had pierced my soul.

"Here. Romans 3. 'There is no one righteous, not even one; there is no one who understands, no one who seeks God. All have turned away—' "[31]

"Sorry. Don't mean to interrupt, but this is good news?" The look on his face should have shut me down, but it couldn't.

"Yes! We fall short, but we're "justified freely by His grace"[32] through Christ Jesus. See? It's not up to us. It's up to HIM! It's ALL Jesus. How did I never see this before?"

"That's great. It really is. Did you say we're having spaghetti?" The Good News was old news to Chuck, who understood it the first time he heard it. It took a tad longer for me; I was catching up.

I struggled to curb my enthusiasm, announcing my weekly findings at the dinner table. "Pouring this cranberry juice reminds me of how Jesus poured out His love for us on the cross."

"Ew! Gross, Mom! How'm I supposed to drink this now?"

"Well, Jesus drank the cup even when He didn't want to, you know."

---

[31] Romans 3:10-12 (NIV).
[32] Romans 3:23-24 (NIV).

The kids' glazed eyes made me want to cry. I had no idea how to pass the faith along to them now that I held it in my hands.

* * *

Maybe it was time to confess. "I'm a terrible mother." I covered my face with my hands. "Lately, the kids don't even want to go to church."

Mom stared down at her hands, clearly looking for words to help me. Then she looked up and shook her head.

"No, Nikki. You're a wonderful mother. One day, you'll see."

Did she see? Did she know that after all her failed attempts at perfection, she was the perfect mother for me? She'd raised the shades to let the sunshine in, drawn my bath, ladled the oats, loaded me into a cozy waiting car, then given Dad the signal to whisk us off to church every week. Faithfully, she'd herded me toward the truth, believing the Good Shepherd would open the gate.

"Honey?" She reached for my hands, and I squeezed hers back, attempting to infuse them with my thanks for never giving up on me. I'd come such a long way; we'd come so far. "I'm so proud of you," Mom said.

"Proud? Why?" If she peeked into the current state of my pantry, she'd take that back. *How can you live with this mess?* she'd say, and I'd have no answer. Because no matter how many times I reorganized the shelves, there was always a straggler that didn't fit.

She held my hands while I fought off her grace. At the core, I was a runner, faker, coward—a selfish brat who pointed out her mother's flaws so no one would see mine. If I could forgive her for being human, why couldn't I forgive myself?

Mom had been there watching my efforts and silently cheering me on. She'd opened the door on my well-ordered and chaotic days, choosing to consider my work brilliant despite being incomplete. Would the housework, homework, or soul work ever be done in the span of a lifetime? No. So, at some point, you've got to consider it good.

Over my bowed head, Mom spoke her highest blessing. "You are a woman of the Word."

Her pronouncement was the most excellent any God-fearing, Jesus-loving mother could bestow on her daughter. I received it because a blessing like that isn't earned; it's a birthright for all who believe. To think I'd almost given it away! There was no turning back now.

The moment washed over me as if I was receiving my fourth and final baptism, with Jesus, Mom, and me wading into the deep sea of God's love. I took one last look at my past and let Mom have the honor of burying my rebellious heart. *In the name of the Father, the Son, and the Holy Spirit.* Divine strength pulled me out of the baptismal and raised me up brand-new. *Buried with Him in baptism, raised to new life in Christ.*

I thought I'd grown up starting my redemption, stopping it, and trying again. But with Mom's blessing came the powerful truth: Jesus had completed the work at the very beginning. My part was to believe that and keep walking it out.

Could we get that preacher with the microphone back? *"Where is Jesus now?" you asked. I have the answer. He's in me. Jesus is in me. I've never been more sure.*

"Christ in you, the hope of glory"[33]—that's what the Word said. Jesus moved into my heart since the moment I opened the door. Every time I ran, He remained. *Because Jesus loved me. This I know.*

Throughout centuries, God's people have suspected this world has "thin places" where Heaven draws near and God's heartbeat is undeniable. I suspect there are thin places between a mother and

---

[33] Colossians 1:27 (NIV).

her child. I've set foot in both at the same time.

Dad entered, unaware he was treading on holy ground. "They're out of chicken noodle, so I got you split pea."

"Thanks, Dad. Hmm. I think they forgot the spoons. I'll go grab some."

* * *

Dr. J was leaning over Mom when I walked back in. He finished his exam and motioned for Dad and me to join him in the hall. His humble demeanor was that of a servant rather than a person in charge. I sensed he knew the latter position was God's.

The doctor chose his words carefully. "Your wife—" He touched Dad's arm. "Your mom—" He touched my arm, then bowed his head and raised clasped hands in something like a prayer pose. "She's in a great deal of pain, putting her body in distress."

As he explained Mom's plight, an alarm went off in the room, urging us back to her side. Dr. J laid the back of his hand on her fevered brow, pressed a stethoscope to her chest, and closed his eyes in concentration, while I willed her heart to keep beating.

Dad held Mom's hand, unable to see beyond his bride's face. He winced when she did, his own tears escaping his notice. This was not the first time he held vigil for a woman he loved. At sixteen, Dad skipped school to hold his mom's hand and wipe her brow while she fought off cancer. In the end, he'd prayed for God to take her, while his eleven-year-old sister, my Aunt Sharon, begged the Lord to let her Momma stay.

Dr. J pulled his stethoscope from his ears and laid it on his shoulders like a mantle. "We can make her more comfortable."

"Comfortable?" Panic rose in my chest while green scrubs and white coats descended on Mom. The feeling I used to have after a childhood nightmare surfaced, only now it was she who needed me, and I couldn't help her. I slumped in a chair, defeated.

Comfortable meant comatose; it was the only way to alleviate her pain. Comatose meant she might not come back to us. I lost count of how often Dr. J pulled Dad aside, shaking his head, murmuring the hard truth.

Mom needed more time. We needed more time. My brother and her only surviving sibling, Henry, were on their way. Since Donnie, her youngest brother, had passed unexpectedly only a few months before, we all knew how quickly life could take a turn. *How much time is enough to say goodbye to the ones you love?*

A definition from Hebrews 11 came to mind. *Faith is being sure of what we hope for and certain of what we do not see.*[34] That great faith chapter, one of Mom's favorites, ended with a list of lesser-known believers, unnamed but honored for their refusal to surrender their trust in God despite all they suffered. They wandered through life in sheepskins and goatskins, poor, harassed, and mistreated by a world that wasn't worthy of them. Some were sawn in two.

No, I thought, *all are sawn in two.* That's what saying goodbye feels like. Only love can endure the bleeding.

"Lynn, honey, I love you so much." Dad's voice broke for the two of them, their dream of growing old together sacrificed for her peace. Grief grinned wide and cruelly on Dad's face, revealing silver fillings that hid years of sweet decay.

Never in a million years had I thought to prepare for this moment.

I couldn't find the words to say all I had to say in a thousand lifetimes. So I said the one word that contained every beat of my heart.

"Momma."

Momma was my first cry, and Mom was God's first answer to the hunger in my soul. Her face was my first look at love. Jesus is the only name in which we are saved. *Momma* was the name that pointed me to Him. Momma poured my Kool-Aid and my bath.

---

[34] Hebrews 11:1 (NIV).

Momma gently scrubbed my back and soothed the sting of the sun on my nose. Momma spread peanut butter on my toast and frosting on my cupcake, carefully wiping up the crumbs. She held my hand tight as I toddled, then gently let me go to find my way.

But Momma was never far. She watched from the window, stood at the bus stop, followed me through the store, then went home to sew a finer dress than money could buy. To Momma, I was worth all the trouble.

I didn't know how to thank her. When I was a little girl, I'd gather dandelion bouquets. Were they weeds or flowers? Only the recipient could decide. Momma took them and displayed them in a jelly jar on the windowsill. But there were no flowers in this plain hospital room, no vibrant signs of God's handiwork.

When people had offered to send flowers, we'd rebuffed them and redirected their gifts toward my parents' home, expecting she'd soon follow. I wished we hadn't. I wanted Momma's last memory of us to be filled with the fragrance of hyacinth and sweet pea and lavender, with the soft glow of fireflies, with the sound of her grandchildren's laughter.

She was the queen of my heart, and like the Little Drummer Boy celebrated in Christmas song, I was empty-handed. What would I offer as she passed by?

Me. Here I am, Momma, unkempt, tear-stained, and wilted.

I stood before her—humbled, unashamed—and let her hazel eyes take me in. I unfurled my arms, and she examined every stitch of her handiwork. It was finished. I'd been torn apart and fearfully, wonderfully sewn back together in a way neither of us could have designed, but this quilt would have the honor of covering her with love one more time.

Dad took hold of Mom's hand. I grasped her other with both of mine. She looked straight ahead and set her chin in brave, godly defiance. What happened to the woman who jumped on a chair when she saw a mouse? Mom was fearless and not done fighting. This was not the end of her testimony but just the beginning.

"Trust in the Lord . . . with all your heart." Her voice rose above the rising waters. "Lean not on . . . your own . . . understanding."[35]

She looked beyond the foot of the bed, the nurse's chart, the ticking clock. I imagined her gaze traveling down the hallways of gurney wheels and rushing feet, past an idling ambulance, over the cracked and frosted asphalt of the parking lot, above bustling holiday crowds, before coming to an abrupt halt.

As she hovered over her grandchildren and all their days to come, every cell in her soul dragged its feet, pulled back, and refused to let them go in exchange for a blurry promise of a dream.

She knew her heavenly Father was good, not unkind, never withholding what seemed best unless He offered better. Jesus must have opened the curtains to the future in that long, drawn-out pause. She would have never agreed to let go of us if He hadn't let her in on His grand plan. I imagined that when she glimpsed the hands of Christ and saw every heart she carried safe and warm within them, her hold on this world loosened.

"In all your ways . . . acknowledge Him . . . and He shall direct . . . your path."[36]

Her face flushed with the effort of speaking, but Mom would not be defeated. Her eyes weren't dark with grief; they were bright with hope. The finish line was in front of her. Her Savior in view, she inhaled a jagged breath on a long, grueling journey. The best was yet to come.

His Spirit filled her battered body with life, and the faith warrior in her rose strong, deciding that she would give the gates of Hell one last shaking. While she had breath, she'd declared victory over the enemy's lies one more time. She took deadly aim and spit in the

---

[35] Proverbs 3:5 (NIV).
[36] Proverbs 3:6 (NKJV).

devil's eye.

"Hallelujah!" she shouted from her cross, her soul finally emptied of fear and filled with eternity. "Hallelujah! Thank You, Jesus! Thank You, Jesus!"

Her face glowed peacefully, a young bride beholding her long-awaited Groom.

"I love You, Jesus" were her final words, spoken before she slipped into a coma.

Her triumph echoed in our ears. The door to Heaven gently closed, and we heard no more, only the rush of angel wings.

Dad and I sunk into our chairs without speaking. Mom had said it all.

My thoughts reverberated with the Bible verse I clung to. *Now we see but a poor reflection as in a mirror; then we shall see face to face.*[37]

I learned that from her.

---

[37] 1 Corinthians 13:12 (NIV).

Chapter 17

Jesus With Skin On

Overwhelmed, I barricaded myself from the outside world. My behavior may have appeared rude, but I regarded it as common courtesy. If I wasn't enough for anyone, I didn't expect anyone to be enough for me. But it was lonely being so polite.

Thankfully, family was on the way to join the vigil. Josh, Holly, and Chuck were en route from the airport. That they'd caught the same flight together caused me to consider whether God, not Chuck's assistant, had arranged the Denver meeting.

I dozed in a chair in Mom's room until awakened by an incessant tapping. It was either family or medical personnel; why didn't they come in? "Coming!" I hissed, joints stiff and nerves raw. I pulled the door open, ready with a "don't-you-know-people-are-dying-around-here" look.

"Sherre?" I stared, dumbfounded, at my friend from church. Did she have someone in the hospital, too? I wasn't used to seeing her without her four small children in tow. I peered down the hall to see if they weren't far behind.

"Oh, Nikki!" She pulled me into a suffocating bear hug. Stronger than me, she practically lifted my feet off the linoleum.

Soon, an explanation met my quizzical look. A thoughtful

neighbor had offered one free babysitting hour for Sherre to shower, shop, or do whatever she pleased. Had I been a mom on a shoestring budget, I wasn't sure I would've made Sherre's decision.

She threw her arms up with a giggle. "When I asked Jesus what I should do, He told me to come here and hug you." So sweet, but didn't Jesus know I was too tired for visitors?

Jesus knows everything.

"Well, gotta run! Mission complete!" Sherre pulled me in for one more hug and whispered in my ear. "I love you so much, sister. I'm praying so hard." After she released me, she speed-walked toward the elevator, calling down the hall. "Could someone please hold the door?"

I collapsed back in the chair, only to hear another knock within minutes. Did Sherre forget something? No, it was Penny. The friend who courageously invited me to BSF dared to love me even more.

Her no-nonsense manner cued to me that this was no social call. Penny was here on divine business. "I heard Chuck's on his way." She pointed to a darkened window in the distance. "If you need anything, I'll be in that waiting room, praying for you until he gets here. OK?" She gave me a curt hug and marched off to man her battle station.

There was a term for what I was witnessing. A clever person coined the phrase *Jesus with skin on* long before I acknowledged its truth. God's loving presence surrounded me in my past and followed me into the present.

I'd often wondered what Jesus looked like, but whatever pretty portraits I've remembered from junior church were probably wrong. The Bible says that there was "nothing beautiful or majestic about his appearance, nothing to attract us to him."[38] Jesus's human skin could barely contain His divine love—a love so captivating that it

[38] Isaiah 53:2 (NLT).

radiated from the inside out and drew all men to Him. His love was alive and well, passing out bear hugs, and dwelling in nearby waiting rooms.

Light from the hallway flooded the darkened room as three shadowed figures entered, bringing both relief and a new wave of sadness. Josh and Holly took turns pulling Dad and me close, then reverently walked up to greet Mom.

"Hey, Mom," Josh said.

"Hi Lynn," said Holly, looping her arm through her husband's.

Mom didn't answer back. It was too late for a two-way conversation. Still, my eyes went over every square inch of Mom's body to detect the slightest stir. If she'd heard the nurse's comments under heavy anesthesia, how much more could her son's voice break through this twilight state?

"She hears us," I decided. "I have absolutely no doubt." I shared Mom's sad experience overhearing the nurse in surgery, which redeemed a former tragedy into a renewed sense of purpose for all of us who had so much more to say to her..

The second Chuck walked in, he wrapped his arm around me protectively, his noblest effort to shield me from pain. In the wake of Mom's last words, I'd become numb anyway.

Josh and Holly stepped back, and Chuck took a turn at tiptoeing through a one-way conversation. "Hey Lynn, it's your favorite son-in-law." His humor didn't move her, but it made us all chuckle—and made me love him even more.

"Have you been home yet?" I asked.

He shook his head, giving a weary smile. "Headed there now. Mom's letting the kids wait up."

It was too late for the kids to stay up, but not really. They had a lifetime of love and laughter ahead. Why wait to start it until tomorrow? Besides, they were in excellent hands. I laid my head on Chuck's broad shoulder and drew the strength needed to go on.

He would've stayed had I asked him, but our children needed his reassuring presence, too. It's always lonelier when Mom's not home. "Tell them I love them," I said. "And Nanny loves them," I added, speaking on her behalf. He promised to pass on the message, then went off into the night. His leaving left me feeling exposed.

Chuck was a shield I hid behind, a refuge I chose over Mom. With his quiet, gallant withdrawal, he removed another layer of all that had come between a mother and daughter, allowing us to draw even closer. I knew he didn't leave willingly. Love never does. Dad's rumpled, unmoving presence by Mom's bedside accentuated this fact.

The clock on the wall ticked away, interrupted by a vaguely familiar silhouette in the doorway. Uncle Henry entered quietly. When he saw his sister lying there, he winced, his heart absorbing the blow. Then he took his place by her side, sitting cross-legged on the floor, elbows on knees, chin resting on folded hands.

Snapshots of Mom with her brothers were rare, and my memories of them were few, yet I had a bent and tattered photo tucked away on the top shelf of my heart for safekeeping. Three children sat in a crumpled row, tousled hair, eyes bright, the photo a rare glimpse into a blurry past I longed to understand but knew I never could. A part of Mom remained there, lost to me.

I looked at Josh, then back at Henry, knowing that siblings who witness each other's pain have the rare ability to see what others can't. With the vision comes a knowing, with the knowing a pact, to keep each other's secrets until it's safe to tell. But that burden is too heavy to bear without a song.

I remembered the sound of singing that had filled my parents' car one Christmas. Despite the Chicago chill in the air and the fact that I wore no seatbelt, I was safe and snug sitting between my two uncles in the back seat. Dad kept his eyes on the busy beltway while Mom frequently turned around to check on me, her smile growing bigger each time she saw her daughter with her beloved younger brothers.

A brand-new children's Bible rode proudly on my lap. Mom had told me the words on the cover were "Living New Testament" and the handwritten words inside were "Presented to Nicole by Uncles Junie and Donnie on December 25, 1970." She called my eldest uncle "Junie" back then, short for Henry Jr., but nothing about him reminded me of my grandfather, especially when he began to sing.

"Silent night, holy night . . ." Uncle Donnie had sung solo until Uncle Henry joined in, the two brothers creating a harmony sweet to the ear. Mom threw her head back and laughed as if she was in all her glory, and I think she was.

I didn't know it back then, but as an adult, I sensed the pain Mom and her brothers carried and cherished that time of singing that served as a living testament of another kind. It was the second-best gift I ever received from my uncles. Was it too late to say thank you?

"I remember you and Uncle Donnie singing in the car one Christmas." Uncle Henry returned my wistful smile, a sadness in his eyes that told me his singing days were over. I didn't want to believe that was true; too many things had been lost to the past.

As the night wore on, our slumped figures formed a perimeter around our fallen comrade. Nurses passed out pillows and blankets and brewed up a fresh pot of coffee at their station. The floor was icy and unyielding, reminding me of the many metal bleachers Mom had parked on to encourage her children and grandchildren. Lopsided scores or double overtime never dissuaded her; she was committed to staying until the bitter end. That her family would now endure discomfort was a suitable tribute for such a woman.

Dr. J entered quietly, making his final rounds for the night. He surveyed the room and crossed flat hands over his heart, visibly moved by the scene before him. Having done all he knew how to do for his patient, he now sought to bring healing where he could. "Dear ones, my home is only a few miles away. Please, come and rest." He opened his arms, pleading. "If only for a little while."

"Thank you, Doctor, but we can't leave her," I said. Dad's nervous chattering had gone silent hours ago making me the spokesperson for the group.

He nodded his understanding. "This love for your sister reminds me of my homeland in Nigeria. May God bless you with peace." He bowed reverently, and the door shut softly behind him.

When hope appears to leave the room, love stays. I don't know how long I slept until the sound of running water made me stir.

"I'm sorry. Did I wake you?" A petite nurse peered around at the shadows slowly coming to life. Her neat blonde bun and fresh-smelling scrubs told me there'd been a shift change while I was sleeping.

I stifled a yawn, looking at Mom to see if anything had changed. Her eyes were closed, her lips slightly parted. Was she breathing, or had she slipped away as we carelessly slept? Panic rose in my chest as I moved closer, furious with myself for falling asleep on duty. The monitor beeped and told me to stop jumping to conclusions. Mom was still with us; I could relax.

"It's OK," I told myself and the nurse. "What day is it?" I'd lost track of time.

"December 12th."

The date rang significant for a reason I couldn't quite put my finger on, a reason outside what was happening in the hospital room. I was thankful the nurse didn't add "Only thirteen more shopping days until Christmas!" Even thinking of the countdown reminded me of the odds against us. The likely fact that Mom and I had spent our last Christmas together was sobering.

The nurse stood awkward and shy next to the sink, unsure

how to proceed with her somber duty. "I'm here to give Mrs. Bliss a bath."

The room's visitors sprung to life, eager to give Mom and the nurse privacy. Joints stiff, Dad and the other men limped out first, nodding their respect to the young nurse. I took advantage of the emptying room, collecting crumpled blankets and pillows, retrieving half-full soup containers and dumping them in the trash.

Mom had taught me to clean up before leaving a room. But she'd failed to warn me that there are times when more is required.

"Would you like to bathe her?" The nurse held the plastic pan toward me.

"Would I like to bathe her?" I repeated, perplexed. I'd been asked that question before. I was twenty-two, barely comfortable with being half-naked myself, when the nurse in the delivery room asked if I'd like to bathe my firstborn. I wasn't like young ladies my age who welcomed any opportunity to put a baby in their arms. People assume all women have an instinct to mother their young, but my instincts told me I had no idea what I was doing. Humans were slippery when wet; I didn't know how to hang on.

Almost sixteen years later, I still hadn't figured it out. People are fragile and easily hurt by attempts to scrub them clean. But sometimes, we're chosen for a job we won't ever be ready for. We have to bravely accept the challenge and roll up our sleeves.

Though every cell in my being protested, I accepted the basin of warm water. Holly, sensing my uncertainty, volunteered to help.

Baths and baptisms are required in this messy life, but only with the cooperation of both parties. John the Baptist initially refused when Jesus approached him and asked to be baptized. "It should be the other way around!" he cried. The honor was too great; the thought inconceivable.

The spotless Lamb humbled Himself and gave a convincing reason. "Allow me to be baptized now. This is necessary to fulfill all righteousness."[39]

Maybe this bath was a necessary part of the healing that had begun between Mom and me. Though her spirit rested somewhere, her flesh continued to wrestle. Love draws near to comfort the brokenhearted, and so would I. Love's warmth would flow over her, cleansing her again with the truth that forgiveness is birthed not through water alone but through the water and the blood.

Holly and I waited for the nurse to leave, then let Mom in on the plan. "Hey, Mom, the nurse left Holly and me in charge of your bath. Can you believe that?"

I took the slight quiver at the corner of Mom's lip as a *No, I can't*. If conscious, she would have never allowed us that privilege. She would've been mortified.

"How do we do this?" I asked no one in particular, with hope Jesus would answer soon. How do you disrobe a human body and not expose its soul? It was a sacred duty I wasn't qualified for.

With my forefinger and thumb, I lifted one corner of the blanket covering Mom. I'd never seen her naked, not once. I'd been told to wait outside of changing rooms while she tried on dresses in department stores. Standing outside, I couldn't help but notice two sets of feet in other dressing rooms, one bare and the other in scuffed and untied saddle shoes. Most daughters were given free admission to a close-up view of their mother's birthday suit, but not me. It had been said that my mother was more than modest and overly shy. Instinctively, I knew Mom's need for privacy had deeper reasons.

I began the bath with her strong forehead, wrapping one finger with the corner of the washcloth to delicately circle her brows and lashes, behind her ears, and under her jaw. Her lips were chapped and cracked, yet a sheer wash of Revlon Red stubbornly clung

---

[39] Matthew 3:15 (CEB).

to them, refusing to surrender the only remaining covering that made her feel well-dressed. I hesitated before applying any more pressure, knowing once that stain was removed, she'd never apply that finishing signature touch again. Mom's lipstick wasn't a matter of vanity, it was her declaration that she would not be defeated.

Slowly, methodically, Holly and I worked, plunging the washcloth into mild water and squeezing out the excess before pressing it to her bare skin. We exposed only the parts of her we had to, quickly uncovering and recovering them with a warm blanket.

Unwilling to let Mom suffer cold, I went back and forth to the sink to add warmth to the bathwater, thinking of how she had done the same for me when I was a girl. I tested the temperature of the cloth before running it between her fingers and underneath each nail. The hands that had so thoroughly touched my life were now limp and unable to reach for me. *It's OK, Momma. I'm here.I'll protect all your secrets. You're safe with me.*

"How do you want to do this part?" Holly's question was loaded. To bathe Mom well, we must wash underneath her gown. We must see and touch all the places she kept hidden from the cruel world by buttoning one more button, stretching a hem down an inch, pulling a robe tighter. I imagined the inner dialogue driving her behavior. *Cover every square inch of your soul before someone can point out your flaws.*

I didn't understand why Mom hid her beauty. It pleased so many people, especially me. When my little legs struggled to keep up with her walking down the aisle at church, Mom turned every head. Like Jackie O, she carried a mysterious air, causing others to assume she had the confidence of American royalty.

But in the privacy of our living room, I watched in horror as she sliced through snapshots of our beach outings, expertly outlining her feminine figure with sewing shears, cutting herself out of my best memories. I only wished I could cut us both out of our worst ones.

* * *

The stranger that opened the door clapped her hands with delight. "She's a little you, Lynn! Don't you think? Henry, doesn't she remind you of your daughter?" My grandfather took a swig of amber liquid and eyed me suspiciously with a shrug.

"Is there a room where we can change?" Mommy asked, ignoring her father's red-eyed stare and smoothing her skirt. The holiday traffic had been extra thick on the way to Chicago, and she wanted to freshen up.

After the hostess showed the way, Mommy wasted no time working to make us pretty. She opened the suitcase, fluffed the Christmas dress she'd sewed on for weeks, and slipped it over my head. Then she switched into a simple green sheath that made her eyes shine and reapplied fresh lipstick with a shaky hand. She bent close, picking a stray thread from my ruffled hem, and placed her hands on my shoulders. "Are you ready to go show Grandpa how pretty you look?"

I nodded and followed her into the living room, trying to contain my excitement. Following in Mommy's footsteps brought praise wherever I went. *Aren't you beautiful! Lovely! Just like your mommy!* People showered us with compliments, especially Daddy. "I'm a thorn between two lovely roses," he often teased, escorting one of us on each arm. Why wouldn't Mommy's daddy say that, too?

"Look at you!" my grandfather exclaimed. I smiled wide, exposing my missing front teeth. I'd never needed to hide from a man; the men I knew were kind. "My, my, aren't you . . ."

Maybe he'd open his arms and ask for a hug. Maybe he'd ask me to twirl around so he might admire me head to toe. Maybe he'd laugh and shake his head in disbelief at his luck to have such a charming granddaughter. Maybe he'd agree I looked just like Mommy.

"You're UGLY!!" he spit out, dashing all my hopes in an instant. Then he threw his head back and roared with laughter.

I ran from his presence. Mommy ran after me and did what she could to cover my shame. She dabbed away my tears, tucked loose strands of hair behind my ears, and whispered love in the nape of my neck. "You're my beautiful baby girl. Oh, honey, I'm so sorry. Grandpa didn't mean it."

But I knew he did.

* * *

Looking at Mom's still body on the hospital bed, I sought to shield her. But how do you cover shame? I'd do it like she covered mine after my grandfather's horrible taunt. Dignity is restored slowly, with small, deliberate gestures that speak to the person hiding inside.

Please don't let me falter, I prayed, pulling the neck of Mom's gown down an inch at a time. I averted my eyes from the port that had infused her with poison, but I was unable to ignore her mastectomy scar. The very place where Mom first offered me her love had been removed, yet cancer didn't stop her love from freely flowing to me in these last days and months. Quite the contrary, our healing had begun.

"We should probably wash her back," I suggested. But I couldn't figure out how to roll her onto her side.

"Here." Holly reached down, wrapped her arms around Mom, and lifted her with a supernatural-strength hug.

Seeing the odd embrace reminded me of hugs at celebrations, then of the significance of the date. December 12th.

"Happy birthday, Holly."

As we bathed Mom, the paradox of the date didn't escape my

notice. Birth is celebrated, death is mourned, and somewhere in between, there's only so much time to bathe each other in love.

I learned that from her.

"Thanks, sis," Holly whispered without disturbing the sacred moment.

Our hallowed work complete, we gently laid Mom's limp figure back down, fluffed her pillow, and tucked the sheets up to her chest. Then Holly and I tiptoed out of the room together, forever changed.

Chapter 18

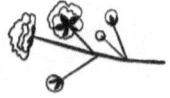

Surrender

It became hard to keep track of hours and days. All things had lost their boundaries, a frightening event for a woman who swore by a schedule. Since the beginning, people tracked days by the sun's rising and setting, but my back was to the window. My eyes were on Mom.

"Is it Friday?" I asked a housekeeper who graciously came to retrieve our overflowing trash.

"Yes. Can you believe it? This week's flown by . . . I mean . . . I'm sorry. Not for you, huh? You have a blessed day now." I looked at the empty trash can. How long before it filled again?

Friday. December 13th. It'd been five days.

Five days ago, I thought I'd wake up at home today, a day I couldn't hit my snooze but would throw the covers off my comfy bed and turn on the shower. I'd have had breakfast waiting when the kids woke up, and two clean leotards and two sets of fresh tights would already have been folded and made ready.

"Are you excited for dance tryouts tonight?" I'd ask Kati, trying to temper my cheery morning voice to match her mood.

While waiting for her answer, I'd busy myself with dishes and lunches, keeping one eye out for her nose to wrinkle or her tongue to peek out of the corner of her mouth. If that happened, I'd casually circle behind her, grab an item from the pantry, and send up a stream of urgent prayers. *Lord, help my baby! Help my girl!*

Jesus had to help her, because I hadn't figured out how to do it right in fifteen years. When she was nervous, I was nervous, and vice versa—a tortuous circle of anxiety made worse by my former B-team cheerleader self, who loved to pop in on this sort of occasion. "You're gonna' be the BEST!" If I could pull off a split-jump at thirty-eight years of age, I would. But she'd probably roll her eyes, so much like me at almost sixteen, but so much better. Kati simply was the best, and it killed me to think she didn't know it.

As the hospital's daytime rhythm took hold, my heart started a new ache. I wouldn't be waiting at the kitchen counter when Kati woke up. She needed me, and I wouldn't be there to cheer her on.

I looked at Mom, lying across the room, her chest barely rising and falling. Did she even know I was here? It wasn't fair. To be a good daughter, I had to be a terrible mother. What kind of mother abandons her child? One that has no choice. I had to trust that Barb, Chuck, and all the other moms aware of my situation would fill in for me. But I wanted to be the one on duty.

Had Mom ever felt torn between two people she loved? I'd never know.

"It's only a matter of time," Dr. J said, gathering his stethoscope in one hand. The monitor lines barely rose and fell. What was Mom waiting for if she wasn't coming back to us?

Outside these walls, life raced by. Inside, it was standing still, barely breathing. Maybe we'd been too hasty to let Mom give up? Maybe if we hadn't she'd be sitting up laughing and shaking her head, thanking God that we dared to say "No, Mom. You're NOT dying. You're gonna push through the chemo and live another twenty years."

Another twenty years! I could only imagine what that would

be like. I'd take the time to let her finally teach me how to swim and sew. We could take a cooking class! How fun would that be? Maybe, God willing, she could see her grandkids marry, then she could hold her first great-grandbaby. I couldn't think about it. To consider that we'd made a mistake with her life was maddening. Was it our fault that she never got her miracle?

After the doctor left, the room emptied until only Dad, Mom, and I remained. Dad stared at the piece of wall above Mom's head. He jumped when I touched his knee.

"Hey, Dad, sorry to startle you. I'm gonna check on the kids. Need anything?" He'd been running on fumes; no amount of coaxing could convince him to leave his post and get a sandwich.

He gripped the ends of the chair to pull himself forward, then fell back, defeated. "I'm good." He repeated the word *good* as if convincing himself. But he wasn't good; none of us were.

I opened the door to find the doorway filled with a larger-than-life man wearing a flesh-colored polyester suit. "Is this Lynn Bliss's room? Is Warren here?"

The man tried to see around me, but I blocked his entry, eyeing him up and down while he hid his irritation with a forced smile. He appeared to be a man on some mission, pushing a utility cart with a square, dusty TV with a built-in VCR. Underneath the TV were a few VHS tapes encased in plastic. The hairs on the back of my neck rose at the look in the man's eyes. I'd seen that look in other eyes before.

"Pastor Bill?" Dad called from inside the room.

The man at the door wasn't merely a man on a mission. This man was on a mission from God. Pastor Bill was Mom and Dad's new pastor I hadn't met. I stepped aside so he and the equipment could squeak by.

I decided to stay while the two men embraced with a stiff hug. Pastor Bill reached to pat Dad on the back and left an awkward hand on his shoulder. I was hyperfocused on his fingers, patting and squeezing my sweet, vulnerable dad in an attempt to console him.

"How ya holdin' up, Brother Bliss?" the pastor asked, ignoring my scowl.

"Okay." Dad's voice broke. The pastor kept massaging Dad's shoulder.

They turned and considered Mom's lifeless figure. "May I?" the pastor asked Dad, not me. Dad nodded.

Pastor Bill approached Mom with a small vial of oil and a handkerchief in his hand. He dabbed oil on her forehead with a finger and pressed it in with the cloth, eyes closed, lips moving. What did a pastor pray in times like this, when faith had dismissed itself from the room?

Soon, another language was heard, the heavenly language I hadn't been privileged to learn. It sounded like a force field activating around Mom, shutting me out of the prayer circle. It didn't feel much like God's love to me.

But I had no love for this man in a cheap suit either. People precisely like him had come between me, Mom, and Jesus and chased me away. This pastor had arrived here from another planet, where God healed you, but only if you had enough faith. He'd come as a missionary for his version of the gospel because ours wasn't working. We did all agree faith without works is dead. But his clear presumption was that Mom wasn't going to die on his watch.

Mom had sat in a pew and hung on to Pastor Bill's every word while clinging to God's, too. Here, she laid motionless and miracle-less. What did the pastor think about Mom's faith? Did she need only a little more to succeed in life? Did she have enough to get to Heaven? I conceded the pastor was there not to dispute the strength of Mom's faith but to give her a little boost to get back in the game.

"It's about the death, burial, and resurrection of Jesus Christ," Chuck often said when laying out his take on theology to random strangers.

My explanation of faith wasn't as smooth; my mind was prone to getting hung up on technicalities. "Salvation is knowing you're a sinner and saying yes to Jesus," I'd begin. "Asking His forgiveness." I'd be walking away when I thought of another thing. "And turning from your sin." Having pulled back from the conversation, I'd run back again. "And calling Him Lord." Later, I'd summarize the conversation in my head. *It's the grace of God, of course!* Why did I have to overcomplicate everything?

Now knowing my salvation was in God's hands, not Pastor Bill's, was a massive victory for me. I watched the pastor's actions from the farthest corner of the room, holding my tongue out of respect for Mom, Dad, and the way they raised me. I'd finally come to terms with the fact that denominations had different takes on the same biblical passages. The truth was black and white. In areas tinged gray by our own understanding, additional grace was required. I fought to find grace in the current situation unfolding before me.

When Mom didn't sit up and leap out of bed, Pastor Bill's prayers went to the next level. His fingers spread wide and gripped the top of Mom's head, shaking his faith into her comatose mind. "Cancer, I command you, in the name of JESUS, to release my sister Lynn! I plead the blood of JESUS! Cancer, you must GO!"

My feet shifted. I was uneasy with conflict, even when challenging a disease that was destroying us all. The pastor was stepping into a position of authority. Did that mean he had to because we hadn't? It felt disrespectful to Dad and God. Shouldn't this be considered trespassing? Struggling with hate for when people crossed a line, I prayed silently. *Forgive me my trespasses, as I forgive those that trespass against me.*

I'm sure Pastor Bill thought I was the enemy, but I wasn't. I would've grabbed a prayer cloth and danced around, too, if doing so would have healed Mom. Given the green light by the Great Physician, I'd have whisked Mom off, buckled her in, and driven her home like a bat emerging from Hell. On the way, I'd have stopped by Video Giant and grabbed every Disney and Christmas VHS in the store. A sleepover the next night had been my plan all along, not this grim deathwatch. Didn't Pastor Bill know I didn't want this?

Regardless of my denomination, I'd have performed any ritual necessary to keep Mom with me. But religion doesn't have that power; Jesus does.

"Trust in the Lord," Mom had said, "lean not on your own understanding." I was doing my best.

"My plans aren't your plans, nor are your ways my ways, says the Lord,"[40] Dad had read, and I was trying not to drag my heels on the journey. Faith was me agreeing with God, not the other way around.

I could never forget that faith and life were gifts, and so was Mom. I imagined the day God decided that Lynn Bliss would be my mother. The Almighty Creator handpicked Mom from a long velvet runner beneath the display glass of Heaven. There were many jewels of all colors, shapes, and sizes to choose from, but His all-knowing eye zeroed in on her.

God pointed to Mom. *This delicate jewel has been created to be worn—* He motioned to me—*in this girl's crown.* All the angels' eyebrows must have raised at that decision. *I know what you're thinking,* God assured them, *but wait until you see how this jewel sparkles in this unlikely setting! Trust Me. It's a perfect fit.*

Isaiah, the prophet who viewed the throne of God, wrote,

---

[40] Isaiah 55:8 (CEB).

"O afflicted city, lashed by storms and not comforted, I will build you with stones of turquoise, your foundation with sapphires."[41] Mom had been storm-battered, inside and out, but Heaven's glow remained on her skin. She was a rare jewel now destined for a more splendid setting than my crooked crown.

One day, my crown and Mom's crown would end up together again, laid at King Jesus's feet. All would be well. All would be healed. We'd shine like the stars forever.

Pastor Bill released Mom's head and slowly walked backward until he stood beside Dad. "I brought some healing tapes," he began.

I wanted to beg Dad not to keep her in this suspended state any longer, but it wasn't my decision. He was her keeper on earth.

Dad's clear eyes didn't see me or the pastor. They rested on Mom and the battle raging there. He'd fight for her to the death, but Dad had more faith than all the worlds combined. Mom was his best friend, his sole companion on a thirty-nine-year journey. He loved her more than he loved himself. Only one Man loved her more; that was Jesus. Dad wouldn't fight Him, even if it meant living out the rest of his years with her laughter slowly fading away.

"No," Dad said, soft but firm. He wasn't angry but wouldn't be challenged.

"You could play them in the—"

"No," Dad said again, even more gently.

"Please," the pastor pleaded one last time, as if he loved Mom more and wanted better for her.

Dad laid one hand on Pastor Bill's arm and offered the door with the other. "Thank you for coming, Pastor." The pastor's eyes were wild with confusion at the unexpected dismissal. He wasn't used to being rebuffed by committed church members like Dad.

---

[41] Isaiah 54:11 (NIV).

My distaste for the man turned to love in that instant. I understood disappointment when God derailed plans. It felt like a slap in the face. It stung. Mom wasn't going to watch my sleepover VHS tapes either.

Like every good Christian girl, I'd hung on to Jeremiah 29:11—"I know the plans I have for you, declares the Lord, plans for good, and not evil." I'd believed it with all my heart, but in doing so, I'd missed the opening of the previous verse. "You will be forced to live in Babylon for seventy years . . ."[42] God's people would travel through seventy years of bad to get to the good.

No one was slapping that exercise in patience on a bumper sticker. To accept suffering as part of a good plan was a high hurdle to clear for a girl who had been taught otherwise. I could only imagine how defeated Pastor Bill felt leaving a parishioner under his care without a victory lap. Mom would be taking one soon, just not here on earth.

I ran to hold the door open, eyes downcast out of respect for this man of faith, while tremendous respect welled up for my dad. Having witnessed his bravest act, I embraced my identity as the offspring of a supernatural love and faith, bona fide holy DNA pumping through my veins.

How had I ever thought any different about who I was born to be? I was Warren and Lynn's child and so humbled and proud. An even greater humbling came from knowing I was a child of God.

I released the door handle. Before it closed, I heard the squeaky wheels of the video cart fading down the hallway.

Dad and I sat in painful silence. What had we done? Did we sign Mom's death warrant? Had we rebelled against God's will for Mom's life?

With his stripes we are healed.[43] I knew that; I'd claimed it a million

---

[42] Jeremiah 29:10 (NIRV).
[43] Isaiah 53:5 (KJV).

times, and so had Mom. Had we claimed it for a millionth time plus one, would that time be the one that worked? The weight of Mom's lost miracle landed squarely on my shoulders. Had I failed her again? *Lord Jesus,* I prayed silently, *show us if we did the right thing.* I was a fast runner and could catch Pastor Bill if I had to.

The door opened, and I jumped up, ready to defend Mom from unwanted intruders. But in walked a very welcome visitor, Dad's youngest sister, my Aunt Sharon.

"Hello," she said with a cheery smile as she embraced my dad and then me in two quick squeezes.

She wasted no time in addressing her sister-in-law. "Hello, Lynn!" Her voice was bright and hopeful, as if she expected Mom to respond. Had Aunt Sharon read the room incorrectly, or was she in complete denial about what was happening? Hadn't she heard how bad the situation was? My mouth hung open in disbelief. Dad touched my chin, and I shut it as Aunt Sharon continued the one-way conversation.

"Oh, Lynn! I can almost hear the angels singing! Can you?"

Mom's failure to respond didn't appear to bother Aunt Sharon. Like Pastor Bill, she laid her hand on Mom's head and stared into her face while she and Mom seemed to have some divine, heartfelt conversation.

When they finished talking, Aunt Sharon returned to Dad. "It won't be long." She spoke the truth with such grace that it sounded like good news.

Aunt Sharon floated out the door the same way she'd come in, with one more hug and two kisses for each cheek. The room was different after she left; it no longer felt void of hope. Jesus had answered my desperate question, and Aunt Sharon had lent us her faith.

God's plans were in motion, for good, not evil, to give Mom hope and a future that would be forever healed and free of pain.

Only God could take what the enemy meant for evil and turn it into good.

I learned that from her.

Chapter 19

Coming Home

Trying to fill in for Mom was almost as challenging as times I'd tried to speak for God. Filling either pair of shoes was impossible.

Mom had given clear instructions to follow in her absence. *No regrets. Enjoy your life. Trust in the Lord.* Those commands clearly based on truth were nonnegotiable. In less-defined areas, I had to offer myself grace.

"Mom would want you to get some rest, Dad."

"You know, I think you were the favorite child, Josh."

"I believe she'd like to keep the shades drawn, nurse."

As I checked my watch every ten minutes that Friday afternoon, there was a more pressing reason for grace. Time was running out for me to make it home to see Kati off to dance tryouts. It was terrible to think that way, maybe downright evil, but if God planned to call His daughter to her heavenly home, why wait until it was too late for me to get to my earthly one? *Trust in the Lord.* Yes, but was He aware that I would have regrets and be unable to enjoy my life if I missed this opportunity to cheer on my baby? Trust in the Lord.

I leaned over the hospital bed. "I'm going to call Kati, Mom.

Her big dance tryout is tonight!"

Perched on a couch in the lobby, I dialed home, expecting the span of a few rings for formulating a compelling mother-daughter pep talk. Chuck answered on the first ring.

"How is she?" I asked.

"Doin' great," he replied in a tone that told me he was obliged to sugarcoat the truth because she was listening.

"Can I talk to her?" Even as I asked, I didn't know what I'd say. *Sorry* seemed too weak. *I'm sorry I'm not there to be your mom. Sorry I haven't washed your tights, checked your bun, kissed your cheek, and whispered "You're my princess." I'm sorry I haven't taught you what you need to know to go onstage without me. I'm sorry. I thought I'd always be there.*

"Hi, Mom." Hearing her voice made my heart physically ache. Oh, how I missed my baby! I hated being held away from her against my will. But I didn't tell her that. I swallowed the lump in my throat and did what all good moms do: I believed all would be well.

"Hi, Kati Girl! Good luck tonight! You're gonna' do great!" My eyes squeezed shut in simultaneous well-wishes and prayer. I'd never forgive myself if she didn't make the team because I wasn't there. "What time's tryout?"

"6:30."

I did the math in my head and considered the logistics. Had she eaten? Was there time for her food to digest? Did she remember to put a backup pair of tights in her bag in case one snagged? I wasn't sure anyone but me knew how to run the washer.

Wait, that wasn't true. One of my epic mom failures may have been helpful after all.

* * *

I'd had enough of the washing, folding, and putting away of barely worn clothes that showed up in the hamper. Kati was ten with an entire decade of experience under her belt. It was time for her to do her own laundry.

"First, sort the darks from the lights. Second, pretreat any spots. Kati, are you watching?"

"Yes. Why do I have to do my own laundry?"

"Because you need to appreciate the work it takes to keep clothes clean. You'll thank me when you're in college."

"I'm ten!"

"College will be here before you know it."

The thought that she'd leave me some day was enough to give me second thoughts on my parenting methods. Was she too young? She should be out in the sunshine having fun with her friends, not in a dank basement working her fingers to the bone. But outdoor fun might cause an impromptu wardrobe change. "OK. Turn the dial to full load and press Start."

A few weeks later, the plan was working. Laundry and guilt levels were down. I was at the apex of motherhood. Then I entered the girls' bathroom to check on Kati and her friend during a field trip. The girls were discussing life from stall to stall.

"Oh, man!" Kati's friend moaned. "I got ketchup on my shirt."

"You can wash it when you get home," Kati said.

"Why would I wash it? My mom does all the laundry."

"Oh." Kati's fallen voice reminded me of when she was a toddler, small and vulnerable. Back then, she begged me to watch *Cinderella* over and over again. Had she ever dreamed that I could be like the wicked stepmother, forcing her to scrub the floors and then locking her in the attic? Maybe she'd had a sixth sense about me.

"My mom doesn't do my laundry anymore," Kati told her friend. "I do my own."

The following day, Kati came home from school to find every single piece of clothing she owned washed, dried, folded, hung, and put away.

Moms are allowed to change their minds. I learned that from her.

* * *

Did Kati know that my love would never change?

"Mom?"

"Yes, honey?"

"How's Nanny? I mean . . . Well, I . . ."

I wanted to fill in the words for her, but I couldn't. How could I tell her the awful truth moments before she went onstage? *Well, my dear, bad news. The one woman who never failed to show up for you will not show up at your next dance.* Instead, I said exactly what Mom would want me to say. "She asked me to tell you she loves you with all her heart and that you're her favorite dancer." The last word cracked, but I cleared my throat to cover.

"Tell her I love her, too," Kati said.

I couldn't speak. *Pull it together, Nikki.*

"Are you there, Mom?"

"Sorry. Dropped the phone. I'll tell her, honey. Nanny and I are so proud of you."

Chuck got back on the line. "Hey, you okay?"

I took a deep breath. "No choice in the matter, ya know? We're holding up here, but I miss you and the kids. So much it hurts."

"I know. We're good here. Don't worry. You're where you should be."

Was that true? If I was where I should be, why did being there feel so wrong? Nothing I could contribute there would change the inevitable. Wasn't I just in the way, another body taking up space, rooting around in faith's pocket for spare change to make sense of it all?

On returning to the room, I passed a nurse's station and detected the familiar melody from an unseen radio underneath the counter. "I'll be home for Christmas," Karen Carpenter crooned. I knew all the words by heart and hummed them to comfort myself, remembering the end of the song too late. Karen was singing about a place she could travel to only in her dreams. I didn't know how much more melancholy I could take.

I took my time going back to Mom's room. What was the hurry? I was only human and couldn't be everywhere at every time. Only God could do that. Family passed me in the hall, heading toward the cafeteria.

"We're taking a break," Uncle Henry said.

"Dad?" I looked for his face among the ragtag group. Of course, he wasn't there. Dad was probably standing guard in the straight-backed chair, sleeping with arms crossed over his paunch, chin on his chest.

"I'll walk back with ya, sis." Josh also must have been feeling anxious about leaving Dad for too long.

When we entered the room, someone had raised the shade and pulled the curtains back to let in the light of late afternoon before the sun set on another day. Dad was standing at Mom's bedside, a blonde stranger's arm around his shoulder.

Outside the window, the sea of asphalt below was coated with fresh snow, reminding me of the white-capped lake Mom had loved to swim in so many summers ago. What did Lake Huron's beach look like today? Cold? Desolate? Was the wind whipping the creaking swings on the playground, to remind them what they were made for? Was the beach grass whispering to the sand and sea, assurance that summer would return once this hard season was over? I wished I could return to a summer day and watch Mom move through the waves once more. I'd jump in and join her without a second thought. But it wasn't to be. My memories would be of Mom in the water and me on the shore, wishing I'd been brave like her.

Even now, my feet seemed sunk into sand, unable to move so I might accompany Mom. Imagining her swimming toward Heaven, I prayed she'd find a sandbar where her toes touched the bottom and gave her rest.

I have no recollection of when the first wave of heavenly reality hit me. I don't know if anyone else lined the shore shielding their eyes from the magnificent sun that burst through the clouds. All I knew was that God's presence overshadowed me in the moment Jesus bent down to lift Mom out of this world's stormy sea.

Every molecule in the air was charged with life. God's Spirit saturated every cell of my body and soul. As that Spirit filled the room, my spirit bowed before my King. *Hallelujah! Glory to God! Thy will be done.*

Before I could fall on my knees in worship, Jesus was already carrying Mom to a peaceful, distant shore. For reasons unbeknownst to me, I'd had the privilege of witnessing Momma's long-awaited miracle, the one she waited for all her life.

It didn't happen as she expected. Do true miracles ever look the way we think? What God promises, He overfulfills in Jesus Christ, His Son.

Momma knew that Jesus loved her. She knew it beyond a shadow of a doubt, because He traveled from Heaven to earth to take her Home, just like He promised.

"She's gone," Dad said.

Death had not stolen her; Jesus had claimed her.

Later, there were many nights I thought back and wondered why Jesus chose the worst moment of my life to make Himself known to me. Had Mom and Jesus paused before making the last leg of her journey? Had she taken hold of His arm with one final request?

Just another moment? she might've asked, knowing her Lord would deny her nothing in His will. How long had she gazed wistfully at my face before submitting her last prayer. *Please let my*

Nikki feel Your love.

Jesus must have said, *Yes, my darling girl. Better yet, how about if we extend the feeling 1,000 generations? Would you like that?* Of course, He knew she would.

Centuries before, the prophet Isaiah wrote, "In the year that King Uzziah died, I saw the Lord seated on a throne, high and exalted, and the train of his robe filled the temple."[44]

Later, I would make a similar entry in the family records. "In the year that Momma died, I saw the Lord . . ."

My heart cried out as the distance grew between us. *Swim, Momma, swim!*

"Thank You, Jesus," I cried in awe of all I'd witnessed.

"Thank You, Jesus." The stranger with flowing blonde hair echoed my praise. Was she a new nurse or an angel sent to confirm Mom's safe delivery?

A holy hush descended. I checked the clock on the wall. Mom must have reached Heaven's shore by now.

There was a knowing in the blonde stranger's eyes. "She's Home. Lynn's finally Home."

"Jesus loves me, this I know." My voice caught as I serenaded Mom one last time for old time's sake. As the last note faded, the blonde stranger—Heaven's messenger?—turned on her heel and floated out of the room, closing the door quietly behind her.

Faith, hope, and love remained.

* * *

Soon, it was time for us to go home, too. I gathered remnants of our excruciating stay—coffee cups, wadded tissues, and magazines—and threw them in the trash. I retrieved Mom's Bible

---

[44] Isaiah 6:1 (NIV).

and hugged it close, hoping to find courage in its pages for the journey ahead. But how was I even going to walk out of the hospital without her?

My steps rang hollow through a winding maze of rushing gurneys, masked superheroes looking up at our family from charts to acknowledge our grief. It felt like we needed to slow down and wait for Mom to catch up. But she wasn't coming, and we had to keep going. I quickened my pace. People were waiting for me at home.

Close to the exit, the soles of my shoes became sticky, and each step took enormous effort. I plodded forward, determined to make it to the door. *Almost there, Nikki. You're going to make it.* I coached my body as if from afar, but I'd never make it if my mind and body fused back together before I reached the door. And I had to get home. There was no other place I more wanted to be.

I remembered the promise I'd heard God make long before I knew what the last seventeen months would hold. *Yea, though I walk through the valley of the shadow of death, I will fear no evil: for thou art with me.*[45] Jesus had been there from the beginning; because He loved me, I wasn't alone. He wouldn't leave me now.

The exit sign was lit up in Revlon Red, Mom's signature color. It indicated the same door I'd entered five days ago, but I was leaving as an entirely different person, forever marked by love. What had once smoldered inside was now set ablaze by witnessing Mom's passing. I was hers. Better yet, I was the Lord's.

If the hospital door should happen to sweep me up in its claws and revolve over and over again, I wouldn't let go of the truth I'd been given. The prayer list that had fluttered out of Mom's Bible month's before now landed at my feet in full view of a newfound calling.

---

[45] Psalm 23:4 (KJV).

Husband

Children

Grandchildren to 1,000 generations

The love and words Mom bequeathed to me urged me on. *Trust in the Lord.* The icy wind outside bit my cheeks, making me shiver. Had my blood thinned? No, my faith had thickened. The cold reminded me that I was very much alive, and I knew, beyond a shadow of a doubt, so was Mom.

That's why it felt strange to leave her there. I pulled out of the parking lot, wondering if Mom felt a similar way when she left me at Camp Faholo thirty years before.

*   *   *

The station wagon's brake lights lit up my hopes. Was she coming back? Did Mom change her mind about letting me go? My heart sank while I watched the lights blink off, then on, then back off again, as the car's tires bounced along the ruts of the camp road leading to the highway home.

With the car out of sight, homesickness entered. I wasn't able to make it through one night without Mom, let alone a whole week. What if I got lost? What if I had another nightmare? What if the zipper got stuck on my jacket or she'd forgotten to pack my swimsuit?

I dragged my feet toward my assigned cabin while laughter and joy I didn't understand erupted around me. Why was everyone so happy when their moms drove away? I opened my suitcase to transfer my clothes to the two dresser drawers assigned to me. One glance at the case's categorized contents told me I needn't have worried. Mom rarely forgot anything I needed.

Underwear, socks, suit, and pajamas went into the first drawer, as Mom had taught me when we practiced at home. After I pulled out the bottom drawer to put the remaining clothes away, an envelope bearing my name and tucked at the bottom of the case caught my eye. Mom's penmanship was unmistakable. She knew I'd be homesick, so she didn't wait for tomorrow's mail call to assure me I'd be alright.

> Dear Nikki,
>
> Have a wonderful time at camp, Sweetie.
> Of course, I'll miss you, but you'll have so
> much fun you probably won't miss me.
> Look for my letters at mail call.
> I'll be back to get you before you know it.
>
> Love,
> Mom
>
> P.S. I'll be praying for you.

Later that week, I'd meet my eventual best friend, Sande, not realizing my first best friend had met me long ago. Mom and I took the long way home to find each other again, hit a few potholes, blew out a tire or two, but we reached our destination safe and sound. Our journey had been laden with what some people call "traveling mercies."

I'd learned to call it the grace of God.

I learned that from her.

* * *

It wasn't until I pulled into the driveway that the equivalent of jet lag hit me. Mom was Home, but I must continue on.

Chapter 20

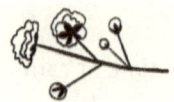

Carry On

"Don't let grief enter your home." That was another one of Mom's last-minute instructions.

"OK, Momma," I'd replied, riveted by her urgency. She knew the despair of being untethered from a mother. But did she know how hard it was to keep grief out once her love unlocked the door to my heart? Every emotion I'd barricaded inside overran my resolve to stay strong somewhere between the porch and Chuck's arms.

On the drive home, I'd coached myself as I had before childbirth. *Don't wail. Don't carry on. Be a rock. Be strong.* Yet I could barely go through life's simple motions due to the pain. I collapsed in bed, wailing in a pitiful childlike voice. "Momma, momma, I want my momma." Once a victorious warrior, I became a scared little girl, the direct opposite of the woman I hoped to be. I was broken; nothing in me worked like it should. I couldn't cook, couldn't care for my kids, couldn't think, couldn't clean. But Jesus never left me alone.

"You should go home, Barb. You've done enough." I pulled a blanket over my head to block the sunlight.

"I'm not goin' anywhere." Even buried under the covers, I

sensed her standing there.

"Do you hear that?" I lifted my head off the pillow.

"What?"

"A car door. Someone's here."

I couldn't dutifully respond to one more person saying *I'm so sorry*. We were all sorry. How many more times must we accept each other's apologies? I dragged my bedraggled self to the front door and opened it. Maybe the sight of an unshowered me would scare off the visitor.

"Debbie?" Chuck's older sister stood in my driveway, a bucket of cleaning supplies swinging on her arm. "What're you doing here?" She lived in Ohio and didn't like to drive.

"I thought you could use some help." She stepped over the threshold and gave me a quick hug before going to work. It wasn't the first time her unique version of grace had arrived at my door to help me.

* * *

I shouldn't be here. I pressed two hands against the walls of the bar's bathroom stall, hoping to keep the room from spinning. This was not how I'd pictured my nineteenth birthday. This was not how I wanted to live.

"Nikki? You OK?" Debbie rapped on the stall door. "Can I get you a water?"

Earlier in the night, I'd begged her to sneak me drinks so I could fit in with the crowd calling me a Goody Two-shoes. I was out to prove them wrong at any cost.

"Let me in." Debbie wasn't leaving, so I unlatched the lock. I tried to focus but couldn't look her in the eye. Did she know how I judged her? She claimed to be a Christian but drank, smoked, swore, and rarely went to church.

At least I didn't smoke, frowned at swear words, and showed

up every Sunday, elevating my Christianity over hers. But as she sat in the stall handing me waters, then led me out into the group with a protective arm around my shoulder, I began to notice the power of grace.

Grace steadies you when your world is spinning out of control if you lean into it.

* * *

There were only a few people I allowed into my neediest times without fair warning. God knew I was too stubborn to ask for help, so He sent Barb and Debbie to demonstrate grace.

That afternoon, when the Bliss family met to discuss Mom's funeral, the grace upon grace I embraced collided with grief upon grief. No one saw the anger approaching; it jumped out in the middle of the decision-making and couldn't be avoided. Grief knocks you right out of your shoes when it hits head-on. I was injured and stunned, but no witnesses came forward to explain what happened. All I could do was pick up the pieces of me and go home.

I pulled away from the wreckage with Mom's lipstick in my pocket but the pearls I gifted her left on her antique dresser. It was okay; I had all I needed to carry on her signature style of grace and beauty under pressure.

My mind was foggy when I turned onto the busy street to go home. A horn blared long and loud before a car swerved past me, its driver waving a middle finger with rage. The silly gesture drove a knife through my heart. Was getting ahead more important than honoring where a person was? I prayed grace upon grace would always lead me home.

On the morning of Mom's funeral, I knelt in the shower and surrendered to Jesus all over again. After all He'd done for me, I couldn't help but kneel. Hot tears mixed with the fresh water running over my shoulders and into the drain. *This is where the rubber meets the road,* God told me, a modern translation of a Bible verse buried in my past.

Jesus hadn't sugarcoated days like this. "You will have suffering in this world," He said before urging his disciples that just because life gets hard doesn't mean you can't endure the hardships. "Be courageous! I have conquered the world."[46]

It was as if Jesus told me, *Your mom trusted Me. It's your turn now.*

"OK, Jesus," I stood up and turned off the shower. There was little time to prepare, but my faith was about to go on a test drive and follow in Mom's footsteps. I'd talk at my mom's funeral as she had spoken at her mother's.

Taking courage from Mom's Revlon Red lipstick in my pocket, I shared my faith while she lay silently behind me with an odd but knowing smile. "Jesus said, 'I am the resurrection and the life.' "[47] That verse seemed an appropriate place to dig in my heels and declare my faith.

Like Mom, I wasn't comfortable standing in front of people. Unlike Mom, I wasn't courageous enough to sing. I did my best to say a few words and trust that it was enough. The index cards shook in my sweaty hands, but I lifted my chin ever so slightly and completed a simple testimony, not expecting I'd ever be finished talking about Jesus and Mom. I was no longer ashamed of my qualifications to speak about the mystery of love. God's grace covered me in all the places I fell short.

Pastor Bill was dressed in a suit more discreet than the one he'd worn to Mom's hospital room. He conducted the service with a few words on our Living Hope, and Pastor Tom sang "Give Me Jesus." I believe Mom and Jesus were pleased with her funeral's display of unity between the Pentecostals and the Baptists, further

---

[46] John 16:33 (CSB).
[47] John 11:25 (NIV).

proving Chuck's nondenominational take on the matter. "It's about the death and resurrection of Jesus Christ."

From my front-row seat, I noticed a glint of gold on Mom's left hand, the brand-new wedding ring Dad had promised her. "Warren, you shouldn't have!" She would've scolded if she could. The old ring suited her just fine. *Like mother, like daughter.* We both preferred weathered, broken-in things that proved redemption was possible at any age.

But to Dad, promises counted. On their thirty-eighth anniversary, he'd calculated the longevity of his wedding vows down to the seconds—1,198,368,000 to be exact. Like his devotion, this promised ring representing his undying love would outlive Mom and him.

At the cemetery, the blue canopy provided no real shelter for the little crowd of mourners huddled around the casket. A sudden blast of arctic air triggered a violent shaking in me that no amount of sport coats laid over my shoulders could quiet. That no one could loiter in such plummeting temperatures for long must have been God's way of gently prodding us forward.

Mom had only two requests for this final moment, both made thinking of others before herself. First, her grave should face east to make it easier for Jesus when He returned to retrieve her body in the rapture. Second, family and friends were not to come back and visit too often, lest we forget that the graveyard was not her home or ours. When it was time to gather again, she and Jesus would meet us in the air.[48]

Yet for those of us who couldn't keep away, she'd chosen 2 Timothy 5:17–18 to be inscribed on her gravestone, the words urging us on.

"I have fought long and hard for my Lord, and through it all, I

---

[48] 1 Thessalonians 4:17 (NLT).

have kept true to him. And now the time has come for me to stop fighting and rest. In heaven, a crown is waiting for me, which the Lord, the righteous Judge, will give me on that great day of his return. And not just to me but to all those whose lives show that they are eagerly looking forward to his coming back again."[49]

The words *not just to me* jumped at me from the page when I looked the verse up in my Bible. Mom's final instructions were etched in stone for 1,000 generations to read and keep true to God.

Mom did exactly what the faithful have always done for those who follow in their footsteps. She left the most important part of herself behind for the next generation to carry with them.

Mom believed an extraordinary life awaited us. Like the biblical Joseph who saw the future Promised Land from his deathbed in Egypt, she knew it in her bones. Joseph's bones and his faith were entrusted to his family, "Carry them with you when God delivers you from here and takes you to the Promised Land."[50] His bones testified of his faith long after he was gone.

I made a vow as I left the graveyard. As long as I lived, I would carry Mom's heart and her bones until it was time to pass them on.

But driving home, I regretted another promise I'd made. "Why don't we have the wake at my house?" I mimicked my peppy voice at the time of my impulsive decision, impersonating the generous, carefree me I hoped to be. As I passed the cars lining my street, I felt like an imposter and braced for the worst. There were more mourners than I expected. Unmade beds and cold casseroles didn't define me anymore, but I still had to face people I didn't know very well, people who might judge me.

I wove through my house like a stranger, unsure of my role. Wary attendees stepped aside to clear a path for me and Mom's Bible, which I'd forgotten to leave with my coat. If they could see

[49] 2 Timothy 4:7–9 (TLB).
[50] Genesis 50:25 (NIV).

inside me, they'd know I wasn't a holier-than-thou Bible-thumper, just a girl who loved Jesus and hung onto His every Word. I set the Bible down on the counter and stuck my hands deep in my pockets, feeling Mom's lipstick and watching the crowd from afar.

A group of dark-haired, lively young people caught my eye. They were cousins I barely knew, children of my uncle who'd passed away a few short months before. They didn't have to come; we would have understood if they didn't. Tears sprung up at the gesture of hours and tanks of gas spent to honor their dad's big sister, someone they probably wished they could've known better.

Should I go say hi? That was the polite thing to do, but it might lead to uncomfortable conversation. *I'm sorry I haven't had any relationship with you for the last three decades. Wanna start now?* The weight of Mom's past laid heavy on me. There'd be time to sort it out—hopefully .

Friendly chatter came from the kitchen, where women buzzed to and fro, refilling cookie trays and coffees, being busy. That's where I felt most comfortable. I'd started to build a stack of half-full plates and discarded pop cans to hide behind when I was discovered.

"Honey, we've got this. Go visit!"

But visiting was where I felt the least comfortable. Forlorn, I shuffled back to my lonely observation deck on the crowd's edge.

Kati and Chapin were cornered by well-meaning adults offering condolences. "Hope your dad has a shotgun!" an elderly uncle joked with Kati. I tried to catch her eye and raise my brows in apology, but she held her own. Chapin was having an animated discussion with a group of Nanny's friends. Neither of my children needed my support.

"They're just like their dad." My mother-in-law came up beside me, carrying a tray of lasagna. "Good with people."

"They sure are," I agreed, but her comment stung a little for what it said about me. How could I make a difference in other's lives without the natural finesse to enter a single conversation? Was I destined to sit on the sidelines with a slice of cake and a glass of punch? When I left this world, what would people say about me? I could almost hear it. *Well, she was a little awkward, but she meant well. She said she knew Jesus but didn't really live it out. God bless her. She's free now.*

Genuine faith wasn't at all what I expected it to be. It wasn't a one-and-done experience. It was coming to the altar repeatedly, not to restart the journey, but to get what you needed to continue. The faith that emerged from the rubble of my past was a long, drawn-out surrender. A godly life wasn't the result of white gloves and pink sponge curlers; it was raw and muddy, a constant wrestling that put hips and noses out of joint.

Some faith springs up from the altar, taking laps while waving its arms and shouting hallelujah. Another faith is more deliberate, making small steady steps toward healing. Perhaps the most faithful among us wake up every morning, thank God for another chance, and limp toward the finish line, believing they'll get there with God's good grace and time.

Like Mom.

Faith rests on Jesus's shoulders, not ours. I learned that from her.

A woman stood alone in the dining room, arms crossed and head down, nervously sipping a Pepsi. *Should I introduce myself? What if I'm supposed to know her?* It was a family joke that I frequently hugged strangers in the store, mistaking them for friends.

She approached me instead. "You probably don't remember me. I'm Beth, one of your brother's army friends. I know Jesus today because of your mom."

The old me would have met her with a polite, empty stare. "How nice!" I'd say, cringing inside, looking for an escape route. But the new me, who had crossed an entire spiritual battlefield with Mom and Jesus in the last five days, embraced my sister in

Christ and began to cry. "Please tell me."

Mom barely answered the door for the Avon lady. To think she had been evangelizing my brother's friends was mind-blowing. What was her strategy? Church invite? Testifying at a dinner party? I leaned in.

"For my wedding shower, she gave me a Bible engraved with my married name." Beth paused to wipe her eyes.

That was it?

"I was so disappointed when I opened it," she confessed. "I thought, 'This is about as useful as the banana hanger I got over there. But how do you get rid of a Bible with your name on it?' "

I totally got that, on more than one level. Once God personalizes your story, you can't shake Him.

"I didn't give it another thought," Beth continued, "until a few years later. We moved often and had a lot of trouble along the way. At rock bottom, I made a last-ditch phone call to my mother-in-law in the middle of the night.

"She asked if I had a Bible anywhere. I found the one your mom bought us buried in the attic underneath years of useless things. My mother-in-law led me to Jesus with that Bible opened in my lap."

I was spellbound. The trajectory of someone's eternity had changed because of a gift not listed on a registry, its giver leading a seemingly ordinary life—a short one at that. I suspected Beth wasn't the only one Mom had pointed heavenward.

"I would've preferred a set of dishes," Beth said, "but your mom had the guts to give me what I needed most. Pretty clever to make it nonreturnable, huh?"

We chuckled, and Beth excused herself. Christmas was coming, and she had five little ones back home. She'd driven hours to pay her respects and deliver that message, because God stories must be told.

Unbeknownst to me at that moment, Mom's gift registry defiance would inspire a future mission for me. Every gift-giving opportunity would be a way to continue her legacy. Many unrequested Bibles would be inscribed with the recipient's name in permanent gold and a generous check tucked in the pages to sweeten the prize, trusting that one day they'd find the true treasure inside.

Beth's story delivered a clear message from God that I desperately needed to hear. Like Mom, I could be myself and courageously take one simple step of faith at a time. Eager to learn more from the people Mom touched, I took a deep breath and waded in.

"Hi, I'm Lynn's daughter. Thanks for coming today." I introduced myself to people from Mom's world and reintroduced myself to people in mine, making sure everyone knew I was Lynn's daughter.

"Your mother bragged about you," one of Mom's neighbors revealed.

"She was always talking about her daughter," a member of a prayer group shared. I decided to assume the best.

"Nicole?" I recognized the rich voice from my past calling from behind me. Rita was in Mom's innermost circle of old friends. When Grandpa died shortly after the Christmas when he taunted me, Rita drove over in the middle of the night and collected Josh and me so Mom and Dad could speed to Chicago. I spent many summers running through sprinklers and chasing fireflies in Rita's backyard. Changing churches had disconnected her and Mom for a while but never changed their hearts, though I hadn't seen Rita in years.

I bent over and gave her a relaxed hug. "Just the person I was looking for. I'm collecting Mom stories. Do you have any I haven't heard?"

"Have you heard the one about when your mom and I went to the county fair and got into a fistfight?"

"Nooo?" Wanting to hear every word, I patted the sofa cushion and motioned for Rita to sit.

"It was such a lovely day. But you know your mom—I had to talk her into having fun."

I loved that about Rita.

"We told your dad and Kenny to watch you kids, take you on a few rides. Lynn and I wanted to sit down and have some ice cream." Her face lit up, remembering. "I don't think I'd ever seen your mom laugh so much, like she was a little girl again, licking the ice cream dripping through her fingers. We were both a mess, but we didn't care. We didn't have a care in the world."

I could picture sunlight dancing through Mom's hair and a scoop of butter pecan melting faster than she could mop it up with a napkin. Best of all, I could hear her laugh.

Rita frowned. "Out of the blue, a terrible fight broke out— two young men shoving each other, taking swings. I wouldn't have been surprised if one of them pulled a knife. Thank God they didn't. People jumped up, trying to get out of the way, but not your mom.

"'We have to stop it,' she said, and before I knew it, she'd pushed through the crowd, grabbed the biggest fighter, and started shouting at him. 'Stop! In the name of Jesus!' She pointed at the other fighter and yelled for me to grab him. I did, but then he got away.

"Your mom's fighter thrashed and screamed like an animal. He yanked her arms back and forth, but she refused to let go. Finally, he stopped and looked down at your mom, all five feet one of her hanging on to him for dear life. He was probably wondering what possessed her.

" 'Jesus loves you,' she said."

Rita paused and sipped her tea, staring out the window with watery eyes.

What had Mom seen in that fighter that made her risk so much? Did she understand his desperation? Did something in him remind her of someone she loved? I wished she could tell us, but maybe she didn't know. Sometimes, the boldest moves we make aren't driven by us. *Greater is he that is in you, than he that is in the world.*[51]

"What'd he do?" I asked.

"He turned his head and kept trying to tug his arm free. Your mom didn't budge and said it again. 'Jesus loves you.'

"A crowd gathered. It was getting tense. Then, the young man stopped struggling and went almost limp. I thought he was trying to trick your mom—that, at any minute, he'd shove her down and run. But he just looked at her.

"'Do you understand?' she asked him.

"I saw her face and arms relax. She must've seen that he understood what she was saying, because she released him, then he ran off into the trees."

I absorbed the scene from start to finish. The entire story happened while I was hanging on for dear life on a nearby merry-go-round. Where was that young man today? After thirty years, was he alive and still running? Or was he sitting up in Glory sharing a scoop of butter pecan with that feisty little Jesus lover who wouldn't let him go?

The latter possibility was likely. When someone loves you like that, you can't keep running. Love never gives up the chase.

I learned that from her.

---

[51] 1 John 4:4 (KJV).

Chapter 21

Letters from Home

Life went on, but never without thoughts of Mom. In the flurry of caps and gowns, college stadium bleachers, and a wedding bouquet tossed over Kati's shoulder, I searched for Mom's face in the crowd. More than once, I swear I caught a glimpse of Nanny, who'd never miss a milestone in her grandchildren's lives. The woman who fought for a front-row seat wouldn't give up so easily.

How does it all work up there on those streets of gold? Chuck had a theory. "What if everyone's already in Heaven when you get there? God's above and beyond time. Why wouldn't He arrange it as if we all took our last breath together?"

I liked that idea. It was hard to imagine but made sense. If there's no pain or tears, why wouldn't we all sit next to each other in the front row, watching our lives unfold?

What would I think as I watched? After all these years of living and learning about God and myself, an uneasy feeling remained around the edges of my faith. God's words and Mom's last words haunted me, telling me that something had been lost in translation.

I'd had a few mountain-top moments like the morning I discovered what Mom meant when she told me to "enjoy your life." I was reading in John's gospel where Jesus's teachings began to confuse and divide the crowd that was following Him so they could enjoy a free meal.

"I live," Jesus said, "because of the living Father who sent me; in the same way, anyone who feeds on me will live because of me."[52]

Frankly, the Lord's use of the word *feed* repulsed me, too. I could understand why people packed their bags, grabbed their kids, and left the premises. But it was as if Mom sat next to me, gently thumped her finger on the word *live*, and turned to me with a curious look. *Hmm*, I heard her say. *Wonder what Jesus said that caused all that commotion?*

Curious, I looked up the Greek word used and its meaning, just like Momma did when studying a passage. The Greek word for "live" was *zao*. Stunned by that word's definition, I plugged it into the verse and translated Mom's cryptic message from years ago. "Anyone who feeds on me will *enjoy real life*."

I would enjoy following Jesus when I pursued Him for who He was, not for what He gave me. Like God's design of a mother and her nursing child, every ounce needed to thrive is found in Christ. But it sounded too simple at times. Jesus was all I needed, but what was I supposed to do?

The day the answer arrived was like any other ordinary day. I woke up, poured my coffee, and dutifully pulled the BSF lesson out of my Bible, wondering what my options were for solidifying my faith at that point. Was feeling like a holy fraud part of the curse?

The lesson's first question seized my attention. "If you could sit down with Jesus and ask Him one question, what would it be?"

I put my chin in my hands and closed my eyes, picturing Jesus's face, seeing the love in His eyes. So many questions swirled between us. Overwhelmed by the task of picking just one, I fought the urge to get up, wash the dishes, and get on with my day.

---

[52] John 6:57 (NLT).

Had I left the question unanswered, I'd have missed the key that unlocked another mystery. Once I committed to the lesson, the answer came rushing at me, knocking me down like a wave rolling into shore, and I wept with relief. I knew what I wanted to ask.

It was a question that hadn't left me since I was a little girl sitting rigid in my Sunday School chair, itching to move but not wanting to disappoint Momma or Jesus. More than anything, I wanted to please them both. I wanted them to be proud of me. I wanted to be good. Grace finally loosed my tongue. Now, I could speak my truth.

I wrote the words in big, bold letters. "AM I DOING IT RIGHT?"

That's all I needed to know. For years I'd been running from that question, spinning in circles, unsure if I was on the right path. While the answer eluded me, I avoided getting too close to people or Jesus, afraid that I'd disappoint them somehow.

The phone rang. It was Dad, one more person I continually let down by my desire to keep moving "Hi Dad, can I call you back? I'm on my way out." Frustrated, I left for the grocery store with the infamous question and my poor dad hanging in the air.

When I pushed our front door open, laden with groceries, I saw an unfamiliar object set on the kitchen table. Dad had been there while I was out, most likely making his daily rounds to check on his family. It wasn't uncommon to return home and discover an article, garden tomato, or antique knickknack he thought I might find useful. Reports of similar findings often came from Kati and Billy, her college-sweetheart husband, and from Chapin, busy living the bachelor life. Beyond loving to gift us with little surprises, I think Dad was hoping to catch us at home.

I made a beeline for the package Dad dropped off, expecting that finding a spot for whatever he'd left would be my primary challenge in my newly downsized home. Taped on top of the floral hatbox was a label that stopped me in my tracks. I approached "Mom's Treasure Box" with reverence. Salvation and children aside, I'd yet to receive a more sacred gift.

"Thank You, Jesus," I whispered. It was as if a parcel postmarked from Heaven on December 13, 2002, had traveled through rain, sleet, and snowy seasons to arrive at my doorstep at the perfect time.

After a long pause and a few deep breaths, I lifted the lid on the box of Mom's treasures. The container was bursting with color from bright homemade cards, crayon signatures, yellowed envelopes, and pastel programs. I drew out the first treasure.

It had all the makings of a card made on a computer, but whoever designed it had taken things to the next level. The watercolor painting on the front, rivaling any found at Hallmark, depicted a peaceful scene of a mother resting in an armchair by an open window, holding her sleeping child. The mother's arms pulled the wee one close to keep her from being chilled by the breeze. The mother's lips pressed on the babe's tousled brown hair, kissing any nightmares away.

Pink floral vines reminiscent of the wallpaper that had once lined my bedroom decorated the walls of the scene. Beyond the mother and child, polka dot curtains swayed off the sill, revealing a peek of a tree, a lake, and a beach. I longed to see the whole picture.

The card looked better than homemade but not quite store-bought. I checked the back for a price. A tiny bouquet of daffodils, tulips, and irises gathered above the card maker's tagline, "Love to Mom."

Curious, I peeked inside, hoping to find heartfelt phrases and elegant words from what I thought might be a note from Mom to Grandma.

Saturday, April 8

Hi Mom,

It's snowing! I thought we were done with the winter-like weather. Hope you are staying cozy and warm. I'm thinking of you. I love you.

Your daughter, Lynn

I'd received warmer messages from my congressman. Still, it was an interesting discovery. Mom calling Grandma "Mom," not "Mother"? And snow in the middle of spring? A gentler season had been on the way, but we Midwestern girls knew better than to pack up the mittens. Seasons and people need time for the frost to melt away.

I read through stacks of cards addressed to Grandma, each with a different picture and message faithfully sent. Grandma must've kept them, and Mom must've retrieved them after Grandma died, perhaps as reminders that even the smallest efforts bring a great reward.

Mom's words in the cards testified to a heart-opening, slow-blossoming forgiveness pushing through a hard soil of hurt, determined to flourish, even through one-way conversation. There were no cards from Grandma in the box.

Another card was sent a year later on Good Friday, the day Jesus defeated sin and death. Although no one understood what God was doing that day thousands of years ago, eternal life was two days away from full, everlasting bloom.

Good Friday, April 21, 2000

Dearest Mom,

I want to tell you that I love you very much.
I know how hard it must have been for you

when Henry, Don, and I were growing up. Mom,
you brought sunshine and flowers to our lives.
May God give you the desires of your heart.
I love you, Mom.

With all my love and gratitude,
Your Daughter, Lynn

Mom had taken extra care to add glitter to the flowers on the front, back, and inside of the card, an extra sprinkle of love sent Grandma's way. One after another, simple acts of faith led to Grandma's future resurrection and planted a seed for Mom's healing. The cards preceded Mom's victory speech on the day of Grandma's funeral. Forgiveness led to gratitude; gratitude led to blessings, which opened a daughter's eyes enough to see that perfect love is never based on performance. Perfect love is yours for the taking simply because of whose child you are.

During our lives on earth, we merely see a reflection of God's love for us in our mothers' imperfect eyes. But we're not our mothers' children alone; we're His. "Can a mother forget her nursing child?" God asks in Isaiah. "Can she feel no love for the child she has borne?"[53]

Sadly, my mom could answer yes to those questions, but God's love outshouts every other kind of love found on earth. "But even if that were possible, I would not forget you!"[54] We are wholly, deeply, and eternally loved from our very first breath to beyond our last.

As they used to say in the pews *God said it, I believe it, and that settles it.* This I know.

But on Good Friday, the cross was violent and bloody, more than some Christians care to admit. Buried at the bottom of the

[53] Isaiah 49:15 (NLT).
[54] Isaiah 49:15 (NLT).

treasure box was a faded envelope postmarked April 8, 1966, exactly thirty-three years before Mom began her ministry of making and sending "Love to Mom" cards. The envelope was addressed to Mom's Aunt Fran.

I remembered visiting Aunt Fran and Uncle Vern at their small airport in the Upper Peninsula of Michigan, hours away from our home downstate. Fran hadn't been blessed with children but had been given the honor of godmother to Mom. Even when I was seven years old, it struck me how Mom clung to Fran when her aunt came out of the airplane hangar to greet us. I'd never witnessed Mom embrace someone like that.

* * *

I took my first plane ride high above northern woods, riding through wet clouds until Uncle Vern pushed down on controls to lower the plane and circle an intended surprise. Below us, a bright teal jewel sparkled in the middle of the thick forest.

"Lake Kitch-iti-kipi," Uncle Vern whispered, "Mirror of Heaven." Uncle Vern dared to fly lower to see if we could make out our reflections. Mom paled, her white skin illuminating her eyes to match the color of the glassy lake below. She smiled at me bravely, her hands pressed on each wall of the tiny plane as if to hold herself together.

"Uncle Vern?" she asked in a sweet, wobbly voice. "Will we be much longer?"

"One more sweep," he answered, executing another dip that left me dizzy.

He circled lower, and I could see specks of people waving at us from below. The wings banked one way, then the other, bringing screams of terror from inside the cabin and shouts of delight from below.

Uncle Vern laughed. "Just a little hello from above to the people below." Until then, I had no idea that a hello from above could be so terrifying.

* * *

Holding the letter made me nervous, as if I was about to experience a free fall, but it was in my hands for a reason. I couldn't set it aside. More troubling, it was written in 1966, five years before we looked into Heaven's mirror. The message sent to Aunt Fran might reflect a closer view of our family than the heart-dropping one we experienced above the clouds.

I unfolded the tissue-thin stationary and read the words of a desperate, wounded daughter. Scribbling on tear-stained paper, she'd tried to articulate the same burning question that had alluded me—*Am I doing it right?*

"I'm not sure what I feel for Mother," she wrote. "I want to say 'love.' But it's almost a pity. I can remember so many things. It's hard to erase memories."

What things, Mom? What memories haunted her and made it hard to love the woman who gave her birth? *Ones too difficult to put into words.*

"I can dismiss some of the things with words like *human weakness, mental illness,*" Mom continued. "But I have the most difficult time explaining her lack of love for me—a mother's love. There was always criticism and so I learned to criticize and be shy. The adult love of a mother for her child was never there. As far back as I can remember, I always thought of myself as older than she—how I needed a mother."

How I needed a mother. I set the paper down, unable to get past that heart cry. *Oh, Mom, I know that feeling. I needed you then, and I need you now.*

Mom confessed feelings she couldn't speak out loud, feelings that must've boiled inside, scalding her from the inside out. "Many of these things weren't really her fault—but I still blame her."

Yep, I thought, involuntarily raising my hand. *That's me. Guilty as charged.* Then there was a line I couldn't fully absorb and didn't want to see. "I blame my father, too. I blame him even more than Mother. Father's been ill, too, for a long, long time."

No mention of her father's absolution followed, but in Mom's eyes, the blame still fell on Grandma's weak shoulders. Mom loved her dad despite the pain he caused. When she received the call that he had died, I stood outside the door, listening to her hellish wails. The grandpa who'd declared me ugly couldn't possibly be a man who inspired more grief than he caused. But love is funny that way; it never stops seeking redemption.

After Mom's funeral, Uncle Henry revealed enough facts for me to draw my own conclusions about the damage done by an oppressive father plagued with demons. But those suspicions lay buried underneath old dirt. There was no good reason to resurrect them other than to spit in the devil's eye and declare the truth that rises above all pain: a precious broken daughter was redeemed by her heavenly Daddy, forever cherished, forever whole, forever safe at Home.

Tucking Mom's letter to her Aunt Fran back into the treasure box, I noticed a whisper-thin scrap of paper the color of buttermilk, Mom's beverage of choice. Time had rendered the words on it almost indecipherable, like her speaking in a tongue that had frustrated and taunted me, telling me that I wasn't good enough or loved enough to receive the honor of a heavenly language.

Without question, I suddenly understood why Jesus gave one gift to one child and a different gift to another. He alone knows what each of us needs to begin to heal. Speaking in tongues was a way Mom could tell Jesus about unspeakable things and feelings she couldn't vocalize.

"The Lord is healing my childhood memories," she wrote. "I cried like a baby. I felt I was telling the Lord things in the Spirit I couldn't speak in English. The Lord is healing my relationship with my Mom. I've been hurt more than angry. Escaping—"

The second page was missing. I searched through the box in vain. According to God's provision, the first page was all I needed to begin another layer of healing in me.

"Oh Jesus, I didn't know," I whispered. But I had known, deep inside. I knew that something hurt Mom so bad that she had to barricade parts of herself from me to try to protect us both.

"Praise God!" appeared on another seemingly obscure page in the box.

"Praise God," I echoed. Nothing is ever wasted in His hands.

I checked my watch. I could dwell inside Mom's treasure box for hours, but if I did, dinner and laundry wouldn't get done. Sure, we'd live anyway, but Mom had taught me better. *Don't leave the little things undone.*

What would one more conversation with Mom hurt, though, before I moved on to my chores? I drew out an envelope as if picking a lucky winner from the day's prizes. Stunned, I read the recipient line, "Mrs. Nikki White, c/o Camp Wolverine."

The postmark was 1999. I'd almost forgotten about chaperoning Kati's sixth-grade camp. How did the letter get in the box? Maybe I gave it to Dad long ago and he threw it in the pile.

I remembered that week at camp vaguely, other than being elected by my group to stand on a chair and kiss a stuffed moose, then experiencing another surprise when someone called my name at the morning mail call. True to her Camp Faholo promise from my childhood, Mom had kept up her duty of sending letters from home while her daughter was away.

January 24, 1999

Hi Honey,

Hope you're having even more fun at
camp than you thought you would. I'm
so glad that you get to spend Mother-
Daughter time with Kati. She must
be so proud—even if she's too cool
to show it. You're such a good Mom
—so involved; it's wonderful.

That January was eighteen months before I received the phone call from Dad that my world was falling apart—that Mom was sick. I had no recollection of reading the letter at camp. I must've skimmed it, then tossed it aside in disappointment, somehow expecting more affirmation. How did I not see the blessing was as plain as the blue ink on the page? It was sent by a loving mother who knew her grown daughter still had a shy, uncertain little girl inside of her, needing encouragement.

Looking back, I was sure I'd been a recipient of similar well-meaning gestures many times over. Had I acted like my eleven-year-old? Too cool to show appreciation? For some reason, I'd failed to see her blessing, because I refused to acknowledge that I was a sinner in need of grace and so was she. This found note was proof that I'd never lost the "good daughter" title like I assumed. I was fully known and deeply loved despite any of my human imperfections. That knowledge alone outweighed a hundred million shiny gold Sunday School stars.

Even more surprising, Chuck had received her blessing, too.

I'm sure Chapin's having a great time
having his Dad all to himself. You and
Chuck are doing a wonderful job with

the kids. Savor every minute, Nikki.
You're building such good memories.
I'll be praying for you.
See you when you get home.

Love Always,
Mom

PS - Too bad about the moose. Sorry.

After I stopped chuckling at Mom's dry humor I missed, I reread the last line of the letter proper again, understanding what I held in my hand really was a letter from Heaven.

"See you when you get home."

When I get Home.

Until then, I had a lot of living to do.

I learned so much from her.

Epilogue

The farmhouse table is set for fourteen, but I'll find room for more. The walls I once built around me have crumbled, much to my delight. Now, one precious voice controls the entire conversation as far as the eye can see, connecting all the dots of our growing family.

The owner of that voice doesn't call me "Nanny." That name is forever taken, so she calls me "Nik."

"Nik, who's your daughter?" I point to her mommy, sitting beside her daddy and glowing pink with another precious girl on the way.

"Nik, who's your son?" I point to her uncle, his chin resting on a ring from a college championship.

"Nik, who's your daddy?" I point to her great-grandpa, Bop, his turquoise eyes back to sparkling.

I watch my granddaughter's blue eyes open wider with understanding.

Then she asks the one obvious question I hadn't expected. "Nik, who's your momma?"

It's been twenty years. With each one, I've grown prouder of the momma I didn't realize I had.

"Nanny. She's my momma. She's not here. She's in Heaven with Jesus."

I say it exactly like I feel it, a hard truth softened by time. But I'm not prepared for the clouds that fill those blue-sky eyes, the sympathy that rains from a little girl's tender soul.

"Oh no. Awww. Do you miss her?"

Eternity hinges on questions like these. Do we dare to tell the truth or keep pretending?

What I wouldn't give to have Mom sitting at this table! I want to see my granddaughters through her eyes, witness all her Nanny dreams for her own grandbabies unfold, and hear her laughter ring through the room. How often I've thought of her singing "Jesus loves me, this I know," while rocking my sweet granddaughter to sleep.

But if things had been different, would I have stayed the same? Some days, I wonder if Mom laid down her life for me. Had she not taught me how to die, I may have never learned how to live. I know I don't have all the answers, but I have everything I need.

"Yes, very much." I confess the loss and see longing like mine in my grandbaby's eyes.

"How did she get to Heaven?"

"She believed in Jesus. She loved Jesus." It's a privilege to share Mom's simple testimony.

"I love Jesus. I believe in Jesus, too." Giving the good confession of faith, my precious curly-headed grandbaby looks so much like her momma when she was little.

And I swear I hear Mom's laughter as a million angels rejoice.

About the Author

Nikki S. White writes "Just a Broken Believer," an inspirational blog for believers who love Jesus but fear disappointing Him.

Nikki touches thousands of people each week with easily relatable posts connecting life in a broken world with God's Holy Word. Her words have also appeared in "A Joyful Life" magazine, as well as served the ministries of "Living by Design," "The Devoted Collective," and "Joyful Life."

She and her husband, Chuck, dwell in her Michigan hometown close to their growing family and the ever-present grace of God. Nikki seeks to live a minimalistic, abundant life with frequent and relentless bouts of heart, soul, and closet decluttering.

Website/Blog: www.justabrokenbeliever.com

www.ingramcontent.com/pod-product-compliance
Lightning Source LLC
Chambersburg PA
CBHW031459120626
46545CB00005B/1673